Souls at Work
An Invitation to Freedom

Praise for Charlotte Ostermann's
Souls at Rest: An Exploration of the Eucharistic Sabbath

"I cannot recommend *Souls at Rest* highly enough, and I would recommend it as the perfect gift for those who may be looking for ways to deepen their faith and strengthen their family bonds."

GENEVIEVE KINEKE,
author of *The Authentic Catholic Woman*

"I love *Souls at Rest*! It is a beautiful book, and I wish every Catholic would read it! It has changed the way I think of Sabbath rest, and the way I approach human *being*, especially on Sundays."

MONSIGNOR VINCENT KRISCHE

"More than a description of and a solution to a problem, Charlotte Ostermann's *Souls at Rest* offers a remedy to busyness and its empty promises. It is an inspiring invitation to come and see what God has planned for you.... This book is an epiphany."

FATHER STEVE BESEAU, Director,
St. Lawrence Catholic Institute for Faith and Culture

"What the world needs now is rest.... Charlotte Ostermann in her book, *Souls at Rest*, drives that home ... with a wisdom, a depth, a beauty ... that makes you hunger for that rest."

SR. SUSAN PIEPER, Apostles of the Interior Life

"God has given us the Lord's Day as a supernatural day in which we can wrap ourselves in the Holy Spirit's *tallit* and truly give ourselves to Him as a bride gives herself to her husband, inviting His indwelling presence to enter more deeply into us. He has now sent Mrs. Charlotte Ostermann to teach us how."

MARTY BARRACK, author of *Second Exodus*

Charlotte Ostermann

SOULS AT WORK

An Invitation to Freedom

First published
by Second Spring, 2014
www.secondspring.co.uk
an imprint of Angelico Press
© Charlotte Ostermann 2014

All rights reserved

No part of this book may be reproduced or transmitted,
in any form or by any means, without permission.

For information, address:
Angelico Press
4709 Briar Knoll Dr.
Kettering, OH 45429
angelicopress.com

978-1-62138-070-2
978-1-62138-591-2

Cover design: Michael Schrauzer

What can persuade us to engage in this ascesis, this labour and this training? . . . It is primarily the *love of ourselves as destiny*, the affection for our own *destiny* that can convince us to undertake this work to become habitually detached from our own opinions and our own imaginations . . . so that all of our cognitive energy will be focused upon a search for the truth of the object, no matter what it should be.

     Father Luigi Giussani, in *The Religious Sense*

Acknowledgements

The way of work does not come easily to me. Without the prayers, good examples, help, and companionship of others, this work would not have formed me, or been formed by me. Thanks especially to Hannah Ostermann, Peggy Shopen, Nancy Yacher, Laurie Robinson, Maureen Murray, Jenny Knight, Emily Beier, Karen Duggan, Kim Rode, Jessica Smith, Betty Thoennes, Father Steve Beseau, Susan Pieper, Stratford Caldecott, Sara Moraille, Laura Hinkel, Terri McLaughlin, Anna Thoennes, Bonita Holtkamp, Paul Haverstock, Karen Barbieri, Robin Carlino, Suzanne Hurtig, and Brother Jerome Blackburn.

CONTENTS

Introduction: Good, Better, Best [1]

1. Write This Book, Please [5]

What Was the Question? [5]—Write This Book, Please! [7]—What is Freedom, Anyway? [8]—Respond, Create Your Freedom! [9]—The Reality Paradox [10]—Notes on Growing Up–One final, optional, preparation for reading this book [12]

FRAMES—Window to Wonder

Notes on Growing Up—Wonder: The Way of the Child and the First Dimension of Freedom [16]

2. Behind the Veil: Person [17]

3. Mediating Structures: The Blastocyst [22]

4. Matrix before Form: The Brain [25]

5. Sacred Order: Holy Geometry [29]

6. Realization: Holograms [33]

7. Waves of Meaning: Sound and Story [36]

8. Architecture of Freedom: Bones [41]

9. Triune Form: Water [45]

10. Windows Through Words: Poetry [48]

11. Transforming the World: Trees [50]

TENSIONS—Workouts for Mind and Soul

Notes on Growing Up—Work: The Way of Youth and the Second Dimension of Freedom [54]

12. Education vs. Formation [55]

Formed by the Potter? [55]—Educated by Experts? [56]—Muddy Waters [56]—You Write This Book [58]

13. Child vs. Adult [60]

Be Like a Child [60]—Grow Up in All Things [60]—So, Which Is It? [61]

14. Work vs. Leisure [63]

You've Got Work to Do [63]—The Weekend–Get Over It [64]—Leisure–The Basis of Real Work [65]

15. Freedom vs. Form [67]

Freedom is Exhilarating [67]—Form is Freeing [68]—Freedom is Hard Work [68]

16. Art vs. Intellect [70]

I'm No Intellectual [70]—But I'm No Artist, Either [71]—Whole Imagination [72]

17. Individual vs. Community [74]

I've Got to Be Me [74]—Do Not Forsake the Fellowship [75]—Your Community Needs You [76]

18. Church vs. Culture [77]
Don't Be Worldly [77]—The Enemy Is Us [78]—How to Build a Bridge [79]

19. Safety vs. Risk [80]
The Risk of Education [80]—Protect Us from Error [81]—Life-to-Life Transfer [82]

20. Intention vs. Attention [84]
Place Your Interest Here [84]—Can I Have Your Attention? [85]—Let's Get Engaged [86]

21. Delight vs. Discipline [87]
You've Got to Want It [87]—But What Does God Want? [88]—How to Win the Tug-of-War [88]

FORMS—Structures Worth Exploring
Notes on Growing Up—Wealth: The Way of Maturity and the Third Dimension of Freedom [92]

22. Maps, Models, Methods [95]

23. Journey [102]

24. Books [107]

25. Classes, Workshops, Seminars [112]

26. Gestures [116]

27. Dialogue [121]

28. Institutions [127]

29. Systems [130]

30. The Church [139]

31. Community [144]

32. The Human Person [153]

Appendix A: Enchanting Education [159]
Charlotte Interviews Stratford Caldecott [159]

Appendix B [170]
The Questionnaire: Charlotte Interviews SAW Readers [170] Education vs. Formation [170]—Work vs. Leisure [171]—Child vs. Adult [171]—Freedom vs. Form [172]—Art vs. Intellect [172]—Individual vs. Community [173]—Church vs. Culture [174]—Safety vs. Risk [176]—Intention vs. Attention [177]—Delight vs. Discipline [178]

Appendix C: The Form of Sabbath [180]

Introduction: Good, Better, Best

IN HIS BOOK *Better*, surgeon Atul Gawande asks what it takes to improve performance. True stories from the world of medicine illustrate the hard-driving diligence, amazing ingenuity, and ethical integrity that underlie best practices and life-saving innovations. His take-home lessons apply as well to musicians, athletes, and saints-in-the-making as to doctors, nurses, and medical administrators.

Improvement is possible. It will not happen without desire, conscious intention, and hard work. Many people will be "low performers," fewer still "awful," most in a murky area I'll call "good." To be "better" requires something saints have always known: self-awareness with a willingness to evaluate one's own performance. In *Souls at Work* I offer you assistance in the formation of your own interior vessel, in moving from "good" toward "better."

Doctor Gawande's experience reveals an interesting relationship between the breakaway, top-performing hospitals and doctors, and the improvement of the many more well-intentioned, well-trained, trying-hard players under the "good" hump of the performance bell curve. The superstars' success is *needed* to spur improvement for everyone in the system. If the bar is not set as high as someone so far has managed to reach, everyone suffers from diminution of expectations, and overall performance drops to lower and lower levels.

Far from intimidating, or shaming, their fellows, the surgeons with great track records, the hospitals that cut superbug infection rates to seemingly impossible lows, the cystic fibrosis treatment center whose patients have double the average life expectancy inspire significant improvements everywhere in the field. Performance improves when someone says "best" is possible. *Souls at Work* is about that movement from good to better to best; from child/beginner to youth/struggler to adult/master; from one- to two- to three-dimensional freedom.

Souls at Work

The spiritual life, unlike the mile run, or the masterworks of Bach, cannot be approached as a skill set or as a mountain to conquer. Because it is woven of your own *being*, practiced in and through your own unique life tasks, pursued for goods no metric can measure, it is difficult to speak of spiritual "improvement" as we speak of performance improvement in other physical and temporal endeavors. What I believe can be improved—with spiritual direction, with conscious attention and effort, with a creative approach—is your capacity for the fullest possible realization of your own humanity, and thus of the space for Christ-within-you.

Growth in the soul's capacity for Christ is increased by sorrow, pain, longing, unrequited love, powerlessness. But these are not means for us to use upon ourselves. There are other means, though, by which you can participate in the opening and deepening of your capacity for Christ. To interest yourself in—literally, to enter *into the essence of*—wonders of Creation, the dynamics of your own struggles, forms others have created to embody their responses to the essential questions you face as you grow: these are means I hope to help you practice using more consciously. You can look *at* things in curiosity when they attract your attention. More, though, you can look *through* things studiously and be transformed by deliberately *placing your interest in* what they have to teach you of God and His ways, of Christ and His way in you.

The saints set the bar for virtue and holiness. They are the "positive shape" we want to emulate and re-present in our own lives. In *Souls at Work* you have a fellow "saint wannabe" coaching your life-crafting and opening a conversation about what it means to grow up, to become free, to be realized, and to practice being you. I've created a workbook that won't really be complete until *you* write it in *your* life. You might wonder, "Where are the 'spiritual' things? Isn't it enough to study theology and the lives of the saints, compare ourselves to Christ, receive the sacraments, avoid sin, and pine for heaven?"

Souls at Work, in its way, goes *beyond* those excellent practices, but in the opposite direction. "Beyond" is not only "toward heaven" but also "toward the rootedness of things in deep, earthy reality." Your humanity—mind, emotions, body, will, senses, desires, needs, and actions—is the natural form upon which the supernatural life of

Introduction: Good, Better, Best

Christ takes shape. The three steps—be present to reality, engage the tensions that reality presents, and enter new forms with responsive attentiveness—could be practiced in any area of work or study. The focus here is upon realities, tensions, and forms from the book written in *my* life. I hope that my set of practice exercises will help you learn to find your own "material" everywhere you look, and to share that with others on this journey toward greater interior freedom.

1 – Write This Book, Please!

What Was the Question?

WE LIVE IN A WORLD bloated with answers. Like diners at an all-you-can-eat buffet, we are coaxed to pile on more remedies, solutions, tips-and-techniques, and third helpings of expert advice. Dessert, if we can force down a bit more, is soft-serve extruded from a 24/7 media machine. The trouble with this superabundance of provision? There's no place in the scheme for hunger—no time to ask the questions.

The purpose of this book is simple: to pose questions only you can answer. These questions will help you participate in the formation of your own soul and of the souls of your children, friends, or students. Consider and answer them for yourself to rekindle the hunger that makes learning a joyful feast. In the process, discover what it means to be fully human, fully free.

Souls at work are souls engaged in the struggle of their own becoming—expanding their own freedom by the exercise of free will, working out the reality of salvation in awe and trembling. They grow—by fits and starts, by discipline and detour—as they explore, stake out, and inhabit the territory of their own being. The subject of this book is You—the free human person who stands at the unique intersection of a particular set of realities. Freedom is a glorious place in which to stand, but you will be tempted to move toward the bondage of less demanding positions.

One of these is the "natural" man, left to his own devices for good or ill, unmolded by the imposition of the will of others upon him. He exists largely outside the social structures of community. Resistant to all authority but his own, he may be at peace with the world or a dire threat to it. At the opposite extreme stands the "contrived" man. Whether shaped to fit a machine's operation, his own favorite image of himself, the demands of a slave driver, or a perfectly homogenous community, he has confined his being to a shape imposed upon him by conscious, external constraint. He may be content with the lot he has chosen or doomed to impotent resentment of it.

In the center stands the free human person—you, the subject of this book. Constrained by truth and virtue, thus capable of living in true community, and not enslaved to external forces, thus free to be fully realized as a unique, unrepeatable human being—the free person is a channel of God's grace into the world. The forces arrayed against you are formidable. At every point in your journey toward eternity, Satan seeks to unmake you—to negate you, to keep you ignorant and impotent. Yet, in Christ you can do all things! In Sabbath rest you rediscover your own humanity, and in working out your salvation you recover yourself—your intellect and fruitfulness. Coming into your own you become capable of the life-giving gift of self, which only a truly free person can bestow. No wonder the enemy of your soul wants to stop your formation, limit your capacity to transmit grace into the world, and crush your desire to be fully and gloriously yourself!

Many people want to reform the world based on some new idea of what a human being is and what he needs. Fewer people are interested in re-forming themselves into living examples of such an idea—struggling to represent in living flesh the ideals they espouse. Even the Catholic "idea of the human person" can become a mental construct toward which we expend the energies of reform while avoiding the need to become a full realization of that idea. When Blessed Pope John Paul II taught that the world needs the recapitulation of the human person, he didn't mean for us merely to make new institutions based on our Right Idea; rather, he meant for us to become, ourselves, *that person* within the context of our own lives. The work of this becoming is the most intensely personal, individual work you can do. As such, it has the greatest power to affect the world unto good—if you will accept the challenge.

Shall we change the social structures—the Church, the schools, the social service machinery, the medical systems, the businesses—for the better? Sure, sure, but first consider one question:

> *How does the fullest possible realization of your own being contribute to the restoration of the world?*

1 – Write This Book, Please!

I hope to help you find your own answer to that question by posing many others.

Write This Book, Please!

Souls at Work chapters can be taken in any order you like. Each one will make a great group study among friends, or for you alone with your journal, with its companion Questions (see Appendix B: The Questionnaire). The sections each take a different approach, so you might want to start by sampling from each of the three. In *Frames* there are wonders presented for your contemplation, to help you recover a teachable spirit. In *Tensions* you'll find paradoxes posed to draw you out of complacency and into the struggle of forming your own response. In *Forms* you and I wander through twelve man-made forms noticing the many ways in which form embodies mind, experience, values, and truth.

Each of the three main sections opens with a proposal that is a distillation of its central message. I hope you will hold that proposal up to the light of your own past experience and of the experience of reading what follows in each section. So, you could begin this book anywhere and benefit from the juxtaposition of your thoughts and mine about whatever topics interest you most—the iron-sharpening-iron effect of thinking *with* another person. To that end, each chapter stands alone and lends itself to dabbling. On the other hand, you could follow along from start to finish, and, for that approach, the Table of Contents is your roadmap. Whichever way you choose, please begin by reading "What is freedom, anyway?" below.

In writing this book, I've tried to imagine how I might take a classroom of willing, interested students through these ideas. My task was to impose order upon a collection of thoughts so as to facilitate the communication not only of a thesis or argument but also of a structure capable of further growth in my readers. Ideally, this would be a conversation between us and with all our friends who are vitally interested in the coming of the kingdom of God into the world. This book is the closest I could come to making space and time for that conversation to occur this side of eternity. I would dearly love to hear your responses and your answers and to watch as you grow and rock the world!

Souls at Work

What Is Freedom, Anyway?

There are many kinds of work we might do in a lifetime, but one of these is accomplished *in* and *through* every other. This book is about the work of becoming free—of cultivating one's own (and thus, others') interior freedom. Both unique (each person's struggle will be different) and universal (*every* person is called to human freedom), the task of entering into the glorious freedom of the children of God is the work of a lifetime. Because this work is linked to your conception of freedom itself—and of theology, work, leisure, personhood, addiction, education, spirituality, creativity, and more—every gain you make in clarifying these ideas is a movement toward freedom.

A proposal is a way of posing a thought for consideration. It invites you to an encounter with an idea that should have some effect upon you, should cause a response within you—a feeling, a reaction, a discomfort even. You first appropriate the idea intellectually, and then you allow yourself the space to notice how it affects or moves you. Then you need to formulate a response to the thought. If you merely *understand* the text, you have not fully digested the proposal. If you allow it to probe your own being and cause an emotional response, you now have a two-dimensional, head-and-heart grasp of what has been said. If you then articulate what it is you feel—what resonates with you, or bothers you, or challenges you, or affirms you in this statement—then you have a three-dimensional encounter with reality that begins to form you in freedom.

Freedom, Father Luigi Giussani has said, is "correspondence to all the factors of reality." In this book, I distill and present to your mind some realities that have affected me and helped to form my own freedom. My hope is that, by practicing this "method" of working upon what you read here, you will increase your capacity *for* all of reality, and thus, for freedom. Learning to enter this struggle—to apprehend, to be affected, then to respond—is the work of cultivating your own freedom. Saint Teresa of Avila teaches these same three steps as a path of prayer—1) you understand your spiritual reading intellectually, then 2) you become present to the affective response of your heart, considering the material in the presence of Christ, and 3) (a crucial step) you make and carry out a resolution that embodies both and engages your free will. Fulton Sheen said, "Free will is a gift, but freedom is a conquest." You create your freedom by every act of freedom.

Respond, Create Your Freedom!

In the context of prayer, your response might be, for instance, telling someone you are sorry, giving a donation to charity, praying for a particular intention, or abstaining from alcohol. Each one of these responses is your own way of taking what you have understood, combining your "head" knowledge with the way this material moves you emotionally, and creating a "new thing": a form, action, or gesture that embodies both—truly carrying out into the world what you possess within your own being.

In the context of this book, your response might be to write down what you sense is the key "take-home" message in each essay. You might go further and create a re-presentation: restate it to a friend in your own words as well as you can; draw a picture or diagram that will remind you of the idea you encountered; journal about the idea and your interior responses to it. Maybe this essay has reminded you of something you need to do, or of a dream you've forgotten to pursue, or of a friend who was just speaking of these ideas. Your response might be to do that thing, to take the first step toward realizing your dream, or to call that friend to discuss the ideas together. When I read, I sometimes respond by writing a brief précis or outline of the material for my own note-keeping and reference. Perhaps there is a quote to send to a particular person, or a thank-you letter to be written to the author, or an online forum where I may discuss the book with others. The response is not onerous "homework" but rather an overflow of my encounter with this particular idea, book, or author.

We often understand, intellectually, the meaning of the words presented to us. Such reading can be helpful in the exercise of the intellectual faculties, but we are aiming here for the deeper formation of interior freedom. If your reading is to be truly "educational," authentically forming your inner being in correspondence with the goal of freedom, then you must take more time to mull over, ponder, contemplate, and be affected by what you have read. This practice can certainly help you develop a more complete "knowing"—linking, as it does, the intellectual faculties with all the resources of the "emotional intelligence" and of self-awareness. In order to cultivate interior freedom, however, another step is necessary: the response.

There is a discomfort in not knowing what to do; in having to wait for an idea to gel into a doable resolution; in finding out that your emotions aren't in complete unity with your intellect; in having a great big idea that you can only carry out in a tiny, symbolic way. It is exactly this discomfort I mean when I say "struggle" or "work" or "bear the tension." This process will result in an act of freedom, and that act may seem so lame that it's hardly worth doing. There is a gap between what you can *imagine* doing and what you can *actually* accomplish. Until you act, you aren't humbled by the reality that it takes real time and practice and effort to fully appropriate a new concept. Without the response, whatever it is, your education in freedom is incomplete. Freedom will remain an intellectual construct for you, and the world of "trees walking" might be all you can see. (Do you remember the blind man in Scripture whose first, partial cure left him in this condition?) Until you create a free act in response to an encounter with reality (an idea, a person, a fact), it hasn't "had its way" with you, hasn't formed in you a greater capacity for freedom.

Reading and discussing ideas with friends is a great path to true learning, for this very reason. The response is built into the learning situation. Friends stimulate us in our efforts to put into words a *response* to something we encounter together. If you don't have a discussion group, grab a journal and write out your responses to share in conversations with friends later. You'll never have to sit through a boring conversation again!

The Reality Paradox

What prepares you to receive Reality? Reality itself. It sounds like an impossible, circular dilemma—like getting your first job with no work experience. But the real world is also a training ground. Just as there are on-the-job training programs for inexperienced employees, every encounter with Reality has the potential both to cause you to hunger for more of it and to enable you to get more from your next encounter.

Far from being an inevitable result of living in the real world, rich appropriation of Reality, or deeply moving encounter with the Real, is every day less likely for someone who lacks this hunger. The words of Scripture seem so unfair: "To him who has, more will be given. From him who has not, everything he has will be taken away" (Luke 19:26).

In this context, these words finally make good sense. He who has little, or no, capacity for wonder, for bearing tensions, for realizing form within his own being will have no way to grasp and retain the marvels of Creation, the depths of truth, or the mystery of his fellow man. He who, tasting and seeing that Reality is good, hungers for more, seeks it out and digs into it, builds the skills needed to fully appropriate it, and allows his own being to be profoundly formed in correspondence with it will receive an overflowing abundance through the kaleidoscope of forms that mediate God's presence to him.

Does it still sound unfair that so much more will be given to one who has much already? If you are tempted to renounce this abundance, or to pride yourself on needing so much less to be satisfied, recall that this is a holy hunger that draws you to your own destiny. You won't be doing anyone any favors to say, at the overflowing banquet table of the Lord, "None for me, please. A crumb of bread will do." He who *is* that all-sufficient crumb seeks to cultivate your appetite for more. You can only *be* who you are, but you are called to greater and greater correspondence with Reality—to freedom.

For you to receive more, nothing is taken away from others. The wealth all around you is available to all and is limitless in supply. Your location, circumstances, interests, and life span limit your exposure to Reality, but you'll have eternity to fill in the gaps in your "education"! Christ—the single Word through which all Reality is made accessible to lowly human beings—has made Himself as small as the smallest human capacity to receive being. As His being grows up in you, your own capacity for Reality grows.

Souls at Work

Notes on Growing Up—
One final, optional, preparation for reading this book

In the course of many conversations I've had and talks I've given based on the ideas in Souls at Work, *an overarching theme has emerged as a larger context for the engagement of persons in the work of cultivating interior freedom. The movement toward freedom happens within the context of the natural process of growing from childhood to maturity. To some extent, then, it "just happens" as naturally as the growth of a plant. Too much self-analysis can be like uprooting tiny seedlings every day to see how they're coming along—destructive! Not enough self-awareness, however, can stunt your growth. At some point, it becomes unnatural for new growth not to occur. In other words, the "effortless, natural growth process" is a good metaphor for your own growth if that process is continuous and you do not stagnate. And if your growth in maturity does continue, then, at some point, you will enter a phase in which hard work and struggle are necessary factors in the process.*

There are three "models" for—three ways of thinking about—the process of growing up that I want to consider. Two, I think, are destructive, or at least problematic. One is the foundation for the thoughts in this book. You may or may not want to see into the "back story" or "underlying matrix" from which Souls at Work *draws strength and coherence. I present it because it has to do with the structure of this book, of the human person, and of freedom itself. Does it surprise you to think of freedom as having a structure, or form? This concept will be more familiar to artists and architects, perhaps. When an idea is realized, we say it "takes form." As it grows more and more fully realized, we say it "grows in dimensionality." When you "create your own freedom," you create a work of art—a sphere of response-ability that is your own particular realization of the gift of, the idea of, freedom. The external manifestation of interior freedom—in your choices and actions—becomes, over time, the work of art we call your life. What "freedom" really accomplishes is the realization of "You."*

Let's look at the two problematic growth models I mentioned and see why they are inadequate for the task of your formation, your realization. I call one the "plant" model, and I have already indicated its major flaw: there is no place for self-awareness, cooperation with God,

1 – Write This Book, Please!

or strengthening of the will. Plants grow, even become fruitful, but they do not become free. Persons expecting to "just grow effortlessly" all their lives are locked into a sort of hyper-child thought system that retards growth. At the other extreme, the "product" model tends toward a hyper-adult mentality in which the person is objectivized, or rationalized, into an inert abstraction. Either way, growth and life are stifled, along with freedom, personhood, and creativity. In our day, the product model seems dominant. We've bought into the idea of continuous linear progress toward a goal (as if a "saint," an "adult," or a "graduate" were a final product generated by a series of value-adding steps along a factory conveyor belt called time).

This model leads to a reductionist ideal of a human person as something that is perfected by being "finished." True growth, however, operates in more of a spiral, or in a three-steps-forward, two-steps-back pattern. We can denote a "child" stage, but we err when we seek to escape childhood, leaving behind its simplicity and dependence. Everyone knows about the uncomfortable self-consciousness and struggle that come with "adolescence," but fewer people understand the delight made possible by learning to reenter this youthful stage at will. Some see "adulthood" as the pot of leisure, possessions, and self-will (or even of holiness) at the end of a rainbow, and they aim straight for it with little regard for the value of the journey itself in the soul's formation. Others avoid maturity at all costs, perceiving in it only a wall of limitation, or a doorway to a meaningless death.

These models, at best, show a person as a "line"—a two-dimensional accumulation over time, tensed toward the end of a short life. At worst, both give us a person who is a "point"—a powerless child or a powerless object without the capacity to wield itself. The model that corresponds to freedom (the "personal" or "global" model) gives us a three-dimensional person, growing up in all aspects of being at once—an expanding sphere with an eternal trajectory. Your dimensions are vast and glorious—so huge is your self, God alone can bear it! As you grow up, He welcomes you into the mansion that is You, realized fully within His being. As you "become free," you grow more and more fully able to inhabit the structure of your own being—a territory veiled in mystery and beckoning with promise. Your own mind can't begin to comprehend the You that He holds: You-the-child, You-the-youth, You-the-

adult, You-in-every-moment-of-life, You-constantly-renewing, You-the-ripple-of-effects, You-the-beautiful-soul. He holds and helps to integrate all the reality-that-is-You into a harmonious unity—a work of art. You cooperate—co-create this freedom-to-fully-inhabit-self—by becoming a conscious, willing participant in the process.

As you live, move, and have being in Him, you move more and more freely within this wholeness that is signified by the word You, or I. You are becoming more "integrated," "whole," with access to the particular freedoms associated with all three stages, or dimensions, of being. The Holy Spirit teaches the soul this full freedom of movement—sometimes seeming to move away (thus drawing her forward as she thirsts, longs for His presence) and sometimes drawing near to embrace (thus comforting and contenting her in heavenly rest).

Look for notes on growing up after each section's proposal. Skip them if they get in your way. You are writing this book, after all, by the way you encounter and respond to it. This book is an invitation to become a soul at work—a person who is consciously growing up in Christ and who daily becomes more whole, more authentic, and more joyful as a result.

FRAMES
Windows to Wonder

Proposed: That reality—facts, persons, nature, works of art—mediates to man God's invitation to freedom. All that can be known of reality corresponds to the human work of knowing in such a way that hunger for, and capacity to receive, eternal bliss are both satisfied and increased by encounter with all that truly is. Each encounter with reality becomes a frame through which your gaze may be focused on a supernatural reality that otherwise would be far beyond your capacity to perceive. Education, at its best, frames, so that we learn to see.

These first essays focus *through* some aspect of reality to the mystery beyond. These are topics I find rich in metaphor, material for contemplation, fascination. Each one has been the starting point for many stimulating conversations, has whetted my appetite to learn more, and has helped exercise my capacity for following wherever wonder leads. As you follow me through these frames, don't forget to stop and be affected, then to respond.

Notes on Growing Up – Wonder:
The Way of the Child and the First Dimension of Freedom

Wonder: the capacity to be stopped in your tracks by reality, to be amazed by something that is, to be affected—even knocked off course —by the very existence of something outside yourself. Wonder is the first dimension of freedom and the characteristic way of the child. Philosophy, worship, humility, and hope all begin with wonder. The soul formed in the context of the kind of "growing up" that pushes past particular realities to abstract ideas is in danger of a body–soul schism. The absorption of self into nature—refusal to distinguish self from other, or to grow up and give honor where it is due—actually numbs the sense of wonder in a different way. The hyper-child and the hyper-adult both miss the tiny entrance into a wonderland of realities that speak to the soul of the highest things and form it to receive them. Your encounter with other persons—with Christ—will be changed by your capacity to be affected by them as realities that lead into a mystery beyond. This capacity is cultivated in childhood, naturally, and strengthened supernaturally by every free act of stillness, of turning to rest in God's presence, of simple trust, of accepting limitation, of identification with place or heritage, of calling out to God for immediate help, of beginning anew. In short, at every stage of life, whatever you do to emulate the child's freedom to receive passively and poetically, to be acted upon, will tend to expand your capacity for encounter with mystery through concrete reality. Wonder is characterized by the feeling of the indrawn breath of delight and by the simple, childlike presence before being.

2 – Behind the Veil: Person

Pope John Paul II has said that what the world needs is a "recapitulation" of the human person, especially of his mystery. The reality of the person is an encounter with the supernatural reality beyond him: his Creator, his destiny, his eternal significance. If I approach an encounter with a person as an opportunity to peek through to the great mystery of Being, then my own capacity to receive persons (and thus, to receive Christ) increases.

Most people do treat others with respect and consideration. Few, though, approach them as a mystery. This is partly because we are busy, distracted, speeding past one another, and separated from actual encounter by technologies that promise to help us communicate. We are trained to look into mirrors and believe that what we see is a purely objective reality. This conditions us to think that, when we see another person, we are seeing him objectively. We are actually trained away from any sense of our own subjective personhood, away from knowing reality as whole persons and not as disembodied intellects. So, we need a recapitulation of our own being in order to develop capacity to accord others their full due as we encounter them.

We can begin by getting in touch with our own needs, desires, weaknesses, and passions. We are told to love our neighbor as we love ourselves, yet we don't often pay much attention to the self as a beloved person. If you learn to be patient with your own growth, you'll be less likely to demand change in others. If you can accept yourself, warts and all, you'll convey that humble acceptance of others. If you can own your own desires and give utterance to things that are hard to say, you'll encourage others to voice their deepest response to reality.

To veil our gaze, according the other a measure of privacy, may seem an odd place to start to see him more fully. The veil, though, is a way of granting him space within our own heart for being, for becoming, for being more than eye can see or mind can quickly grasp. The gaze of love veils another person in much the same way a reference beam that helps generate a holograph interferes with the stark appearance of an object under a direct, overhead beam. In *Till We Have Faces*, C.S. Lewis made powerful use of the metaphor of the veil.

Lewis's retelling of the myth of Cupid and Psyche reveals new dimensionality in the Christian understanding both of myth and of the human person. The pre-Christian myth, like the pre-Christian human being, is veiled in a darkness that constitutes a reduction from an ideal—a flattening of the fullness of story, or of person. Lewis retells the myth in the inescapable light of the Incarnation, and in doing so he illuminates and revivifies the notion of personhood, as expressed through its characters.

In the original, Psyche goes to be married, but in *Till We Have Faces* she goes to be eaten. Simple human consumption is transformed in the new tension between an evil that would consume humanity and a total self-donation that would rescue it. In *Till We Have Faces*, as in real life, the stakes are much higher, the tension much greater, than in the unilluminated world of myth. The original Orual, Psyche's less attractive sister, is motivated by jealousy, whereas Lewis's Orual is motivated by a longing that she can only hope conforms to its object, and she must walk by faith instead of sight. Lewis chooses a first person, subjective narrator, Orual, over a third person, detached or objective narrator. His retelling is intensely personal, as is the "true myth" that fulfilled all mythology on the Cross. Mythology's Psyche acts out of fear and delusion, but Lewis's Psyche acts to save Orual. His characters are all more complex and less two-dimensional than in the original myth.

The story of characters within time, straightforward and somewhat flat, gains three-dimensionality as Lewis has the original myth told by the priest within *Till We Have Faces*. Orual's participation in Psyche's redemptive tasks adds layers and folds to the fabric of the story. In the light of true myth, the material of the old myth is quickened into life and fullness without at all Christianizing the pagan world in which it occurs. In the same way, elements of our pre-Christian lives take on dimension, fullness, and sacramental

2 – Behind the Veil: Person

meaning once we enter the new life, the new world created by the Passion and resurrection of Christ. Lewis also adds to the sense of personal dimension by giving his story witnesses—entirely missing in the original. These others remind us that persons are only fully developed in the fullness of community, of a "cloud of witnesses" in which the glory of human *being* is borne. Without the living mirrors around us, and the Living Mirror in whom we are seen wholly, we too would be "characters" somewhat flattened and distorted—lacking the capacity to convey any story but our own.

Beauty, for the old storyteller, was a curse. He rightly divined that, sought for its own sake, it led to death or deformation of the soul. Lewis boldly makes beauty the goal in *Till We Have Faces*, rightly divining that it points to something higher and that as such a symbol it has sacramental power in addition to its power to become an end in itself. In his Christian understanding, he places responsibility for the right use of such awesome powers as man wields squarely back upon the shoulders of man. No more would "the gods" be responsible; rather, a free man with a free will would choose what he would and would not see when offered truth, beauty, goodness.

The original myth conveys the false dichotomy of the pagan world. The world was reduced to more manageable size by a black-and-white sense of good vs. bad. Again, Lewis's retelling takes risks and adds dimension to story and person by returning to the world a capacity for paradox, tension between seeming opposites, the risk of truth. Dark and light, rationality and imagination, I and Thou stand no longer in opposition but rather in creative tension within the Lewis version of this myth. It is tempting to read it through the old, simplistic lens of "either-or." In a two-dimensional reading of *Till We Have Faces*, Fox—the Greek slave who tutors the sisters—could be seen as rational (i.e., non-Christian) and therefore "bad"; Redival—their promiscuous younger sister—as sensual (i.e., pagan) and therefore "bad"; Psyche as beautiful (shorthand for "good" in easy stories); and Orual as "ugly/bad".

Lewis offers us the chance to see through the veil of his story to a more complex understanding of these characters, and hence to a richer comprehension of human beings in general. Fox is a stunted rationality. Separated from his "Greek-ness," he does not follow

Greek thought to the antechamber of Christian faith. Reason fully developed would have led him to the "unknown God," but intellect divorced from the fullness of life left him in darkness. Redival is a stunted pagan—all sensuality, ignorance, and vulgarity with none of the wonder, awe, and appreciation for beauty that, as Lewis believed, brought true pagans closer to the experience of God than some Christians. She has life in the created world, in the flesh, but the glory of it is wasted on her. Psyche was beautiful in the sense of the ideal, but she needed the physicality, the help of Orual's companionship in suffering, to *real*-ize her beauty in its fullness. With goodness, with truth, her beauty became three-dimensional, but not by her own strength.

Orual represents Lewis's own coming-to-grips with the tension of paradox—the integration for him of rationality and imagination, mystery and enlightenment. The possibility of flawed love that he considered in *The Four Loves* is resolved in her as love is cleansed, darkness exposed, and beauty revealed beneath a veil. As a character, she is rich and deep and human and true. Her personhood is not violated by a simplistic rendering of her struggle but rather is veiled in a way that speaks of the Christian understanding of human dignity. Lewis allows her to reveal herself, to be exposed only as she is ready to bear the truth about herself—and then only to the gods and by her own free will. While she staggers under the weight of the frightening, dark aspects of herself, we realize through the story that it is her openness and love for beauty that has exposed her soul to the light. While she labors under the burdens she must bear and sees her weaknesses exposed, we see the healing power even of her struggle. This is not a salvation by works but rather the integration of her being through work, writing, struggle, journey, and self-sacrifice.

In the end, Lewis has transformed the flat landscape of Cupid and Psyche into a world of texture, dimension, light and shadow, depth and height. The centrality of the New Man—the three-dimensional, illuminated, incarnational understanding of the human person—in this story gives it its tremendous power to speak to the reality of our being. In the stark light of the pagan mythos, a person is a story and perhaps a symbol. Unveiled, exposed, vulnerable, he accepts the fate of his life and takes for himself what pleasure

2 – Behind the Veil: Person

he can. In the light of atoning, redeeming, sacrificial love, this person is transformed into a sacrament, a vessel of glory. Veiled in dignity, exposed only by his own free will, able to exchange his suffering for the good of others, he accepts the noble mantle of a Christ-bearer and retakes for himself the dimension, freedom, and dominion of personhood.

In many ways, in the world around us, the veil has been removed. People allow themselves to be debased, exposed, and vulnerable to being treated as objects. Not only immodesty in dress but also immodesty in public self-disclosure and the disintegration of norms of behavior take heavy tolls on the dignity of the people around us. Somehow, our attitude, our gaze, our response must seek to restore, in some measure, a dignity that many people don't even realize they have relinquished.

When a sign as powerful as a human person has been robbed of meaning, only our own sense of that meaning can restore, can refill, the sign. By according persons a high level of dignity, mystery, and significance, you lift them to a more fitting place within your own heart. Who knows how much of this treatment it would take before someone "feels" a difference or begins to manifest transformation, but the reality is that you have this restorative, raising power because of *your* greatness as a human being, the image of God you bear, and the Christ you re-present in encounters with others. Such transactions lift you up, too—out of the shallow flatness of typical interactions.

When you approach another person with awe, with delicacy and deliberation, with openhearted hospitality, and with a capacity to be fully present to him in the encounter, the presence of God is mediated to you through him. The more you experience this, the more amazing the people around you will become! We'll consider persons again later, as three-dimensional forms that invite you to enter, to exercise your freedom, to experience the mystery, and to respond. Each of these frames is, of course, a three-dimensional reality that moves us to wonder at, to struggle toward, and then to enter the mystery of, Christ. If you can learn to stop and wonder, all frames become doorways.

3 – Mediating Structures: The Blastocyst

WHEN A NEWLY CONCEIVED PERSON has grown to only sixteen cells, there is a pause before its growth resumes after attachment to the uterine wall. When I read this—about the "blastocyst" stage of human development—I felt a thrill of excitement. This little fact caught my poetic imagination. The "pregnant pause" or "expectant hush" is known in poetry as a caesura—as essential to a poem as a rest is to music or negative space is to the composition of a still life painting. Without stopping to get a degree in cell biology, I read on, hoping to understand even a small part of the science of blastocysts.

Apparently, during this pause, walls between the outer eight cells morph into the structure that will become the placenta—linking maternal and infant bloodstreams after implantation of the child in the womb. What captivates me about this is the image of the microscopic baby yearning and moving toward the matrix of support. God has designed *me* to move forward toward my destiny—my own needs, desires, and emptiness correspond to the fulfillment that lies ahead, ultimately in Him!

The placenta is a "mediating structure." Both baby and mother give up something of "self" to build unity with the other. Within its safety, the waiting cells are quickened and the child begins to grow again. (My own motto is *semper incipe*—always begin; no wonder I love the way this image affirms our need for new beginnings, even from our earliest days!) God has said "yes" and has called. The child has said "yes" and has come. The life of the mother and child (like my own life within the Church, so richly prepared to receive and support me) are unified and interdependent.

Life-to-life transfer begins with the exchange of blood between a baby, who simply waits to become, and a mother, who yearns for the day when they will meet face to face. Somehow, hugeness and smallness are made one by a structure that does away with their differences, establishing the perfect proportion between them. Without a

3 – Mediating Structures: The Blastocyst

mediating structure, the mother's blood would flood the baby's microscopic capillaries—overwhelming their capacity to assimilate.

The blastocyst has implications for education—certainly a life-to-life transfer, at its best. As a mediator between student and reality, formal education must prepare the student to outgrow its protection and face reality on his own. His own desire must be engaged to bring him into the "middle world," where he may taste, absorb, and appropriate reality in small, but nutritious, doses—reduced in size, but not in quality. I began to see my home as the next "placenta" on my children's gradual journey toward adulthood. My "diet" enriches theirs. My attention to my own needs and desires helps me to be a better "mediating structure" for them. They meet whatever and whomever I love through me and start seeing the world through my eyes!

When I consider the delicate structures that must form to give an embryo access to maternal riches, I have to remonstrate with those who accuse the Catholic Church of being merely an "organization" instead of a living "organism." In light of the blastocyst, I doubt whether any structure could be more perfect than the Church for raising us to fullness of life. Her history of defending believers against enemies and errors reminds me of the individual cell wall—a semipermeable, highly organized (and amazing) mediating structure. The water balance in a single, almost invisible cell affects a whole person for good or ill.

That leads my thoughts to grace—the "water." I see that I can become "dehydrated" if I fail to thirst for the constant movement of grace into my soul. Scientists have learned that water is important not only because of the materials it carries into the cells but also because its presence balances the individual cell's interior state with the exterior context of the whole body. Grace, likewise, is the gentle proportioner between my interior state of being and the exterior context in which I exist. The graces of God are, themselves, mediated to me through the Church, through the sacraments, through prayer. I see that the mediating structures, far from being an empty context, are themselves of critical importance.

The tiny blastocyst, then, has led me to a consideration of all the structures that stand between me and reality, between me and other persons, between me and God. I want to think about whether they are all as well-designed as the placenta that unites mother and child.

It has been said that television is the real educator of modern children. Certainly, television shows (and similar media, such as movies and YouTube videos) mediate reality to kids, teach them norms of behavior, and respond at some level to their perceived desires and needs. As a mediating structure, though, how trustworthy is this technological "placenta"? Looking back at the blastocyst, I think of the child as reaching out, wanting to touch the "real" world and connect with it. He turns on the television and the one-way flow begins.

Already I see a problem. The set can't respond to his needs, can't help buffer him from sensory overload, can't protect him from toxins, and can't change the flow based on his response. Perhaps an attentive parent is accomplishing these functions; if so, the television will affect the child differently. I worry about the extent to which media train and manipulate desire and need such that they become stimuli for automatic, programmed behaviors—making the viewer less rather than more free. How are you regulating what you "ingest" from books, movies, television, and other media?

There is a sense in which the child must take in, must digest, reality—his mother, his world. The image of the newly conceived child beginning to do this, having the impetus and power at such an early stage to begin this activity of interacting with reality, simply amazes me and leaves me in awe of the mystery that is the human person. I see through this tiny window my own task of becoming, of reaching out to establish connections with reality, and of appropriating and re-presenting it within my own being.

4 – Matrix before Form: The Brain

THE HUMAN BRAIN is one of the wonders of the world! Everything I learn about its structure and the way it functions gives me new insight into the mind of the Creator. When I think of the vast, interconnected matrix of wisdom that God created to support all the forms of Creation, I see the brain's interconnected synapses, and when I consider the synapses, I'm reminded of Holy Wisdom. Reality emerged through this wisdom as form, and it now emerges through a similar network into my own mind.

Truly, I am *capax omnium*—capable of containing the universe, in this sense! Its Creator, perfect *Being*—the I Am—has deigned to enter the space-time continuum as material substance through which I may see and know Him as He—over time—is realized through my neural substance into my very being. I love this! The brain organizes my consciousness, or sense of self, along three planes that have correspondence with the dimensions I perceive to be an aspect of my being. From the center outward, from right to left, and from back to front, my brain works to create and hold onto a coherent map of who I am, where I am in space and time, and what is true about my personhood.

I am one tiny point of particularity in an incomprehensible array of possibilities, yet this amazing brain somehow orients me, helping me to establish a dynamic balance—creating a stable frame of reference that I may carry with me. God is the originator of the very idea of "me," and this means that my brain was given a womb-like capacity to nurture that seed, growing to accommodate it and giving my own ideas a similar space within which to become realized. My brain seems to support, without encompassing, a hologram of "me" as the eucharistic host carries a (much-more-fully-Real) Presence that transforms it without eliminating the need for it.

Like Christ, the Head of His body, the Church, my brain is the all-knowing harmonizer of the symphony of nerve impulses, hormones, and cellular messengers in my body. The hemispheres of my brain—verbal left and imagistic right—speak to me of the Word's coming into a pagan, mythopoeic protoevangelion prepared to receive Him, and dependent upon Him to voice the world's deepest needs. I picture the Just Judge seated upon my corpus callosum (the interface between left and right brain) rendering compassionate judgment to reconcile two ways of "stating the case"—integrating and balancing my being and my body's competing claims for attention.

By such judgment I am set free, restored in my capacity to bear tension and generate creative response. The critically important glial cells (once thought to be mere filler, without function) remind me of the Sabbath space for nonaction that sustains all the "doing" of weekday work. I read about metacognition with avid interest—thinking about thinking, and about how much metaphor helps to build the infrastructure for my understanding of the world. Each image-in-word creates new links, new pathways for understanding and expression. My brain's nature is to know-in-words, verbalize its knowing, resolve tension through word and story, create word bridges to reality, icon-paint the world in image-words. Every approach to the mystery of the brain is a moment with the One who is Word. Could there really be any doubt that I was created in His image?

That my intellectual powers are resident in, and dependent upon, brain tissue for their being does not diminish their fascination for me. Memory, for example, far from being a mere electrical charge or chemical reaction, is of great importance to the whole sense of self. For people without memory, the coherent hologram of self fractures into unconnected particles of yesterdays. I thank God for a Church with a coherent story that enriches my story, and for history lessons, photo albums, family traditions, and Scripture that all support my sense of memory.

As I watch the development of a child's brain, judging from his outward actions what stage he is passing through, I think of the brain's hunger to know—to investigate and categorize and experiment with reality, so that every encounter (even the scary ones!) becomes true food for the enrichment of his brain. What capacity

4 – Matrix before Form: The Brain

does my soul have for the Food it is given? Truly, to him who has much, more will be given!

I marvel at the multilayered convolutions of the brain. It isn't very pretty, but it is "capacity" concretized—growing by every link of self-with-self, every new unity of concept-with-word, and every experience of internal sensation linked with external phenomenon. Connections of all kinds increase the strength of my mental matrix—ideas shared, unity with other persons, "aha" moments when pattern and meaning are discovered.

The brain seems to thrive on work. "I" inhabit it more and more fully over time, though I only manage to take on about 20 percent of its potential capacity. I slowly dawn upon myself, much the way I gradually awaken to the fullness of self that God has held ready for me in His own being since my conception. My brain is, in some sense, a symbol of the Church. The Self of Christ is realized within the organized structure that holds together all the unities of persons who make it up. Within my brain, words are the "organizing principle" and images the raw material of experience.

Recent research into the mirror neurons of the brain has revealed the connection between these neurons and language development. Watching the people around him, a baby performs some amazing feats of unconscious mimicry. His brain physically conforms to the pattern of speech he is hearing and seeing from others. The attraction of faces and mouths for a baby springs from the hunger his brain has to gather up and possess the world—facial expressions, sounds, gestures, spatial relations. The brain yearns insatiably not just for "input" but for this vital bond between self and other by which a child begins to find himself, literally, within the gaze of those who give him place in their hearts, eyes, arms, home, and being.

The implications of this mirroring activity are enormous. Marco Iacoboni, neuroscientist and author of *Mirroring People*, worries about the impact of media violence on the natural, imitative dynamics of brain development. Without active mirroring, a person may lose a coherent sense of self, become incapable of empathy, and fail to develop the capacity to receive others into his being. Even motor development can be adversely affected by problems with mirror neurons, which should be firing to prepare specific muscles to "practice" all the physical events a child observes. Autistic kids may be experiencing mirror problems, and some are already being helped by therapy that strengthens mirror neurons.

All this is fascinating in itself and also as a help in understanding what Christ meant when He said, "Abide in me, and I in you" (John 15:4). If you gaze into His eyes, you will see yourself there. Love has held you in His being since your inception. If you follow yourself, and follow this Friend, you are sure to move toward your destiny, to become more fully *real*-ized and free, because the One who allows Himself to be a lens through which you look toward heaven is also the One in whom you live, and move, and have *being*.

5 – Sacred Order: Holy Geometry

It is fascinating to explore the treasures God has left for us to find within the very geometry of the world around us and in the system of numbers that corresponds to it. You do not have to be a high-level mathematician to appreciate the way these "secret" correspondences and symbolisms were discovered and wondered at by pre-Christian people.

The circle, for instance, has long been used as a symbol for all-that-is, for perfection, for God. When ancient geometers used a compass to construct a circle, they thought of that as three-part action (without any understanding, yet, of the triune nature of God!): point, reach, and sweep. *One* could only be described in this triune way: the circle's center, its radius established by the reach of the compass, and its circumference drawn by the compass's swing round the center. When they drew two circles mirroring each other, amazing things began to happen!

The two center points established the endpoints of a line—an expression of two-dimensionality. From the one-point to the two-point perspective, a new tension was created, and a "vessel" seemed to be formed in the overlap of the two circles. This vessel was an almond-shaped space that seemed to be yearning for resolution of the tension—open and waiting to be filled. You will notice the *vesica piscis* (fish-shaped vessel) or *mandorla* (almond-shaped vessel) as the shape of the glowing area behind the image of Our Lady of Guadalupe and in many, many works of sacred art and architecture.

When the geometers connected the endpoints of the line with the pointy end of the "almond," what do you think was formed? An equilateral triangle! In their words, the form was "born" through the *vesica piscis*. This form seemed to emerge into the world from a universal ideal of perfect balance, stability, and strength. There are many examples of triangles used all around you to give structures strength—in nature and in man's works. Even America's three-part government was designed for stability and strength.

Once you begin to look at the wonders of number and shape, you see them all around you. When you study the unique perfections of the triangle, you may be so amazed you can hardly continue into four, five, six… much less the "virgin" number seven, with its mysteries, or the blessed eight of perfect rest (and of the musical octave, and the glories of the periodic table!). On and on it goes, every number, every form holding treasures for us in a mathematical "language" that St. Bonaventure says is "the principal exemplar in the mind of the Creator," and which leads to wisdom and delight in beauty.

As an image through which the form-of-trinity entered the world, the *vesica piscis* is also rich with Marian symbolism. The aura of holiness and the manifestation of the Holy Spirit's work in the world radiate His beauty and perfection. The open unity poised between the Old and New Testaments, between longing and fulfillment, was offered as a vessel for the resolution of that tension. In the womb of re-creation, the future forms (all derivative from the triune form) were present, as all those in His body are given place within Mary, our Mother, and in Mother Church.

The number three is pivotal in the history of man and of number. It is the first number that can be represented in the "real world," the world of knowability, without adding to its dimensionality. One and two were considered, for this reason, the "parents" of the number three—ideals impossible to realize as forms. (Draw a dot to represent "one," but it will actually have three dimensions, no matter how tiny; likewise with a line, as the molecules of ink add depth to the length and width that your drawing describes.)

Then, three is the last number capable of full realization without diminishment of its dimensionality. (Try drawing, or sculpting, or building a representation of "four dimensions," for example.) Before the Trinity entered the fallen world as form, myths and religions could only approach the fullness of Truth, waiting for resolution of man's interior tension *toward* God. Since the "birth" of the form *of* the Trinity, all other forms and religions are derivative, partial representations, fractured subsets of the Catholic Church.

5 – Sacred Order: Holy Geometry

If I could make one book required reading for Catholic parents and educators, it would be Stratford Caldecott's *Beauty for Truth's Sake*. In six succinct chapters, he leads readers from the history of education's disintegration to a vision for its restoration and "re-enchantment." Caldecott's proposal to return wonder, beauty, integrity, and, thus, enchantment to the sphere of education calls for a reawakening of some ancient sensibilities.

Modern man has been uprooted from the very ground of his own being—the Word of God expressed as number, proportion, and form, which undergird Creation's beauty and his own. His awareness of sacred symbolism has been dulled by the divorce of poetry and pedagogy. He comes to the study of philosophy and theology not prepared by music and disconnected from history. He suffers from the deformation of the liturgy, and in his flattened state he has lost capacity for interior freedom. "The keys to meaning are (and always have been) form, gestalt, beauty, interiority, relationship, radiance and purpose. An education for meaning would therefore begin with an education in the perception of form. The 're-enchantment' of education would open our eyes to the meaning and beauty of the cosmos."

Caldecott would restore to us the interior spaciousness expressed in the great medieval cathedrals by the interplay of light, space, "stone and statuary, rose windows and labyrinths" in the service of sacred liturgy. With Plato, he believes that "the inner vision of the soul could be awakened" by the disciplines of arithmetic, geometry, astronomy, and music. He would reintegrate the liberal arts curriculum by locating it "within the history of ideas."

With the Christian Pythagoreans, Caldecott explores the "logoi of Creation ... understood in terms of number and cosmic harmony." Beauty, he tells us, is "the key to the lost unity" of subjects as diverse as "art and literature, music, mathematics, physics, biology, and history." "I want to immerse us in an alternative vision of mathematics. . . . The Pythagoreans regarded each number as an expression or facet of Unity (the Father of all things) projected through Duality (the Mother) to create multiplicity."

We live in a time characterized by "a severing of the intimate bond between cosmology and ethics, facts and values, but with a changing sense of the self." The key to the restoration of civilization is worship! "But if we are to renew our civilization by renewing our worship, we must understand also that liturgy is a way of being in tune with the motions of the stars, the dance of atomic particles, and the harmony of the heavens that resembles a great song. And Catholic liturgy takes us even deeper than that. It takes us to the source of the cosmos itself.... When we come to Mass...we should be able to experience a sense that here, at last, all the threads of our education are being brought together. If we don't something is wrong with our education or our liturgy."

Liturgy is the "lost key" not only to "humane education" but also to "the reintegration of all things, all subjects, in a vision of sacred order." Liturgy recalls us to the expression of gratitude: "The more grateful we are...the more beautiful we will try to make the gift [of self]. That is partly why liturgy has always inspired art." Caldecott sees the art of courtesy as a vital channel for this same spirit of gratefulness. "The elemental courtesies of conventional etiquette and good manners are the vital channels for preserving this spirit in everyday life. [An] education that actively cultivates such modes of behavior will begin the process of building a society that is liturgical to its very core, in which the 'air' of grace can circulate. Harmony of soul can only be restored through effort, and the restoration of manners and kindness is an important beginning. Without it, little else is possible."

We must recover the fullness of our own reason, which involves knowing by both "head and heart," through the soul's reason (*ratio*) and the spirit's (*intellectus*). "A third dimension has to be introduced into cognition itself, otherwise faith will appear entirely extrinsic to reason." Education à la Caldecott aims to restore "ontological depth" to a flattened universe on the way to a human person with three-dimensional freedom. His introduction to the symbolic cosmos, sacred geometry and number, golden proportions, and storied stars should be required reading for Catholic educators, scholars, parents, and priests. (See my interview with this gracious man in Appendix A.)

6 – Realization: Holograms

HAVE YOU SEEN a hologram? It's a two-dimensional image that looks amazingly three-dimensional. In the original Star Wars movie, a recorded holographic image of Princess Leia is projected with her verbal message into three-dimensional space. There is a hard-to-counterfeit hologram on US dollar bills. Nothing produced by modern technology has so captivated my imagination as these visual mysteries. Here's my understanding of how a hologram is created.

There is an object in view that you wish to re-create as a hologram. Begin by shining one light upon it from above, which illuminates it as fully as possible. Call this the "object" beam. Now choose another point from which to shine a steady light upon it, and call this the "reference" beam. From your object (let's call it a "vase" so as not to confuse the two uses of the word "object"), light bounces off and would transmit an image of the vase to the eye of a viewer or to a camera, but you want more.

So you place your film at a point where the interference of the images generated by the two beams will be recorded. Each light source, each bouncing line of photons, carries in itself the shape of the vase—is bringing back to your eye a wave deformed by contact with the vase in such a way as to bring a three-dimensional representation into your optic nerve. When the two waves intersect, a confused pattern is formed, called the "interference pattern."

When the film is developed, a strange picture results that can only be "decoded" by a third beam—a laser "development" beam. When the interference pattern is developed by this third beam, instead of just handing you a two-dimensional, confused image, the final print is, voilà, a holographic representation that looks like a three-dimensional object! If that were all, it would be pretty interesting, but look at that hologram to see more wonders. If you cut that print up, each piece of the hologram contains a complete, smaller, three-dimensional image of the original vase. The interference pattern is "developed" over the whole surface of the paper somehow (for the life of me, I can't fully grasp it!). The body of Christ is, in a sense, a huge "hologram" of Him. He is whole, if smaller, in each one of us, but the glorious reality is the Whole—the fully realized image of God only possible in the unity of those of us who bear His image.

Now, what does this say to me about "seeing" three-dimensionally? This has helped me put words to my experiential understanding of human relationships. First, the "object" beam—that which reveals all in stark clarity—reminds me of the Father God's all-knowing, inescapable, from-every-angle apprehension of a person.

Next, the fixed "reference" beam reminds me of Christ seeing the paradox, the "both-and" of me-as-I-am and me-as-He-created-me-to-be. I realized, then, that when I look at other people, if I seek merely to know all the facts about them, to bare them to my scrutiny, I am "playing God" and imagining my own viewpoint as capable of an omniscience that, thankfully, is possessed only by God Himself.

When I see someone with the eyes of Christ, or through the lens of His love for them, they are, mercifully, veiled to me to some degree. It is at this point that loving becomes full of struggle. How much easier to see them "one-dimensionally," flattening them for my convenience by labeling, tucking them away as a neat mental construct. But to see them in all the confusing "both-and" quality of the "interference pattern" is to struggle with the—often negative—effect they have on my own being.

I am affected, moved, touched. I am tempted to give up and ease that tension by deciding for myself which aspects to focus on and which ones to ignore. But the Holy Spirit reminds me to invite Him into this interaction. Only the Spirit can bring to this tension a creative resolution that violates neither of us. When the "third beam" shines into the interference pattern, I see a glorious new thing. As much as it is possible for me to do so, I see a "three-dimensional" human person—one who not only can affect me but also has the depth of unspeakable mystery and can be a window to the mind of God (for, of course, God "resolves" all the confusing, contradictory elements of each person's being perfectly).

6 – Realization: Holograms

My desire is to help people develop the capacity for the wholeness of others, the interior freedom to bear tension and allow the Spirit to "do a new thing" with the reality we encounter. When I think about Christ taking up a fixed position (a particular man, born in a specific time and place) in order to "interfere" with perfect justice by adding to it perfect love, I am better able to bear that tension myself.

In C. S. Lewis's *Till We Have Faces*, the veil is a significant element. You can "veil your gaze," your knowing of other people, by refusing to "objectify" them—that is, looking at them with only the stark light shining to expose faults and deformities. Only God should be in that position, and Christ's steady reference beam reminds you to look through His eyes instead, with His love for another person and His humanity. If you then feel somewhat confused, even frustrated about the contradictions of what "is true" and what love sees in this person, you can realize that you have not invited the Holy Spirit to "develop" the image. You are trying to "resolve" the interference pattern yourself, and you simply cannot do it without God's help.

Just as an image of a vase can be filled with much greater dimensionality, Christ *fulfills* the Law of the Old Testament, His coming is in the *fullness* of time, and He is both *fully* human and *fully* divine. Through holograms, you can get a better grasp of how a space of time, a legal form, a man, or a small wafer can be the same thing it ever was yet now be more *full*, more richly imbued with whatever is of the essence of, or is central to, its *being*.

7 – Waves of Meaning: Sound and Story

WHAT DO SINE WAVES and stories have in common? It was a big surprise to me to find a link between them. As I learned about the form of sound waves, described with the aid of trigonometry's functions, I realized a correspondence that signified a wonderful mystery to be explored. Sound waves can be shown graphically by machines that translate them into a visual image—paper rolls under a stylus dancing to the tune (as your tiny ear bones would vibrate to translate sound into nerve impulses).

The "picture" of a single vowel, or a sonata, can thus be taken and analyzed mathematically. What we see, depending on the complexity of the tones, is a wave pattern rising and falling symmetrically, resembling rolling hills or jagged mountain ranges. If the sound stays steady (say "Ah"), you'll see a grouping of peaks and valleys that repeats, like a wallpaper pattern, every so often. If it varies, the "repeat" may be harder to find. If, instead of varying consistently, the sound just keeps changing erratically, there won't be a visual pattern. Instead, you'll have a picture of random noise, with no repeats.

Now, all that is fascinating enough, but there's more! The long wave image on your strip of oscilloscope paper consists of a series of less complex waves that are added together to form the image you see. One sound *adds to* another, literally. If sound wave X is made up of waves A and B, then at every miniscule point along its timeline, it represents the addition of the two waves at that moment. If A goes up when B goes up, X is as high as their combined amplitudes—the sounds amplify, or magnify, each other. If X (and the sound of a single vowel may take several wave formulas to describe) is the unique voicing of all the component waves that construct it, then its shape is a realization of them all at once, in unity. (Are you excited yet?)

I was struck by the way this new "language" spoke to me of story structure. Let's back up just a bit. A simple song could be said to

7 – Waves of Meaning: Sound and Story

have a basic pattern repeating several times in succession (a hymn's verses repeating four times, for instance) and thus an overall not-very-high, not-very-low shape with few different peaks-and-valleys that resolves within a fairly short span of time. The pattern of a complex piece might repeat less frequently, taking much longer to resolve, or complete one cycle.

A listener is in tension, to some degree, waiting for resolution—of a chord, a symphony, an expected pattern, a loose end. Just like a story, right? The typical description of a "story arc" goes like this: characters in a setting experience crisis or conflict that is finally resolved. There may be a longer or shorter lead-up and a longer or shorter denouement; there may be mini-crises and multiple stories woven together for greater complexity. This is the basic pattern we expect for the "form" we call "story."

Describing story as layers of sound all additively resulting in the final form seems much richer to me. This metaphor gives us inaudible waves of back story operating at the low, slow, inaudible frequency of deep history's "bass tones" below the story we "hear." Each character's "wave" is unique and has its particular impact on the whole, no matter how small. "Story" begins to resemble "symphony," and so does "life," at this point. Like a soprano descant detached from the full choir, or a person with no sense of memory or heritage, story-made-of-fewer-waves is "thinner," less full-bodied.

How different your self-concept will be if you realize the depth of "story" from which your story emerges, and the heights to which it aspires! This image helps explain why God is not "using" us or "pre-destining" us when He works all the realities of all people over all times together into the unimaginable symphony of His story. You can't think of sound without considering music.

When I hear, in Oliver Sacks's *Musicophilia*, that musical memory helps reconstitute the *self* in patients with severe brain disorders, memory loss, and Alzheimer's disease, I am not surprised. My son's organ teacher once told me that music has an "architecture," a dimensionality that is only fully understood experientially. This quality of spaciousness, of actual place-making, seems to be unique among all the varieties of sensory experience. Music is singular in its power to knit together the self—memory, intellect, emotion, imagination—into a hologram of being within the mind. The heart-mind, or ensouled mind, thus given realization is, apparently, beyond the brain's strictly physical capacities, and consequently it persists in some persons even when the underlying neural structures have been badly damaged or destroyed.

Studies have demonstrated music's power to rouse the emotions and to intensify associated memories. Mice have responded disastrously to heavy metal music and have thrived on Mozart—stunted, asymmetrical neurons resulting from the former and long, lovely neurons from the latter. Plants prefer beautiful music to noise. Babies seem to gain in responsiveness and inquisitiveness under the influence of classical music. There is clearly something wonderful about music.

Just as it takes some degree of preparation and maturity to "bear the tension" of very complex music, your capacity to hold on hopefully, waiting for a far-off resolution or for complexity to emerge as pattern—in life, in reading, in a scientific experiment—must be cultivated.

To the extent that I write my own "story wave" (at least, the middle tones that fall between the way-high "sounds" of transcendent meaning and the way-low "sounds" of hidden history, which all go into my makeup), I amplify or stifle the sound that God wants made in this moment. I may be really very inept (hopefully, I am not willfully "deconstructing" His design!) and repeat some bumbling patterns at high frequency until I grow more "in tune with" the Conductor. I probably have my share of moments when my own "sound" is interfered with by others', and then I must trust God to weave all sounds together for my good.

There is something wondrous to me about the way sound resonates, the way it causes vibration and correspondence in other places, persons, ears, and hearts. Faith comes to me by hearing the Word of God. The Word of God is to dwell in me richly, resounding through me. There is a directness about sound that gets right to the core of my "I." Josef Pieper, in *Only the Lover Sings*, describes music as "wordless jubilation" that moves directly upon the core of the soul with an intimacy that is unveiled by the drapery of words.

Just as a story must have some setting in which to "take place,"

7 – Waves of Meaning: Sound and Story

sound must have a chamber in which to resonate. It cannot be heard in a vacuum, because material, the stuff of air, is needed to carry it, conduct it, mediate it to my ear. A disembodied idea cannot be realized in a vacuum without concrete means. A story must be communicated via words, characters, dialogue, paper-and-ink. This necessity of means is a very Catholic concept. Atheists prefer to assume the reality of our existence as a given, without reference to a Giver. Protestants prefer the idea of a universal body of Christ to the (messy and imperfectly realized) reality embodied in the Catholic Church.

What are the means by which God is mediating Himself to you, and mediating *you* to the world you encounter? What song is He singing directly upon the waters of your soul?

The image of human beings as resonating chambers for the Word of God reminds you that the enemy of your soul wants to silence you. If a person can be kept from contact with reality, kept from being affected deeply, and kept from authentic and free response, he is effectively silenced. Too many things to count seem to have this very agenda of shutting down the person as a place of encounter with being.

Let's start with that contact with reality. How many interactions do you have with real nature, real music, real need or pain, real people in physical reality? If your whole life is becoming "virtual," you are being silenced. How are you kept from being affected? The more you are buffered and protected and detached from reality, the less likely you are to be affected by it. The more your heart is hardened to emotion, to empathy, to compassion, the less likely you are to be affected. The quicker you can speed past something, the less likely you are to be affected. If you cannot allow what enters your mind to sink in deeply, if you cannot wait to attend to your own response, then to some degree you are being silenced.

And last, how are you kept from responding? Sadly, as people speed past you, you lose the opportunity to respond. As you are "freed" from courtesies like thank-you cards, reciprocal invitations, and opening doors for others, you lose many more opportunities to respond. If you are among those who are losing the power of words—the power to take meaning from and put meaning into words—you are gradually being silenced. If you are a slave to social dishonesties, saying only what people expect to hear, you violate and silence yourself just as well as an enemy could wish. If you are hesitant to sing, you cut yourself off from a rich interaction with the one "musical instrument" made by God specifically for ease of use and profound interpersonal connection.

Gladly, the Church continues to invite us to the musicality and rhythm of her liturgy. Not only in the organ music or the chant itself but also in the call-and-response movements, the poetry of a psalm reading, the choral speech of the recitation of the Creed, and the music we absorb unconsciously from the sacred geometries expressed in architecture do we participate in the being-moved-to-respond and the resounding-of-the-word that is music. Choral singing is a rich image of life in the body of Christ. Members of the choir or the congregation express, by making their unity a chamber for the play of sound, the full dimensionality of parts in harmony with whole, members unified under one head, the Church in heaven and on earth in collaboration to resound the praise of God. Theirs is an elevated "language" that contributes to the epic dimension expressed in liturgical speech.

Without music, something is missing that is deeply human, deeply humanizing. Formation in words, in prayer, in contemplation, and in music are intimately related. If you are a-theistic, you are not oriented toward belief in God. If you are a-mused, you are not oriented toward and not formed "by the muse," the mystery, the encounter with transcendence. It is no wonder most of our silence occurs while we are "not musing" but instead while we are merely being oriented toward shallow absorption of the messages and music that hit us from every side.

The musical, poetic nature of the human person—his interiority, his capacity to resonate with truth and beauty, his wholeness, his vivid dimensionality—is highlighted by the view through the frame of "sound." To experience the fullness of this dimension, we need to learn to appreciate well both silence and music. If you will stop to wonder at sound, you'll discover much, much more in the territory beyond that simple frame!

8 – Architecture of Freedom: Bones

THE HUMAN BODY is full of material for contemplation. Look no further than your own structure to increase your capacity for wonder and awe! The bones, in particular, fascinate me. I find in them an image of the law of God—to be interiorized as virtue and animated by love through Christ.

We take for granted the freedom of movement we are afforded by this internal skeleton. Imagine how encumbered we would be with exoskeletons large enough to cover "beetles" six feet tall! If nothing in the design of man is "accidental" but rather is integral to our existence as bearers of the image of God, what do these bones have to teach us?

As a parent, I create an exterior law, hoping my children will internalize it as they mature. Their muscles are meant to develop and, in the process of pulling those bones every which way, to strengthen the bones, too. I've got to let them use those "muscles"! They must be allowed to make some choices, take some falls, have some freedom. If I keep an external cast on too long, the muscles atrophy and eventually even the bone declines in density.

The opposite scenario is no prettier. If I let a kid with a broken bone walk unsupported, greater damage—even deformity—may result. It's dangerous to keep him locked in the "safety" of legalism, but it's also dangerous to set him "free" with weak formation, with no moral guidelines or supervision. So, bones have helped me learn to be a better parent.

I enjoy everything I can understand about the way bones serve as little factories for blood cell production. I'm no osteo-expert, but just knowing that this is happening deep within the structure of my being reminds me that there is life-giving wisdom in the old laws given to the Israelites. The empty space supported within the matrix of bone marrow speaks to me of Sabbath rest—the leisure, the openness to the Spirit's interior infusion that keeps the burden of bone, law, obligation from becoming too heavy to bear.

I've learned that the joints—so necessary for fine articulation of movement, for gracefulness—are particularly vulnerable to injury and inflammation. I approach carefully the transition points—the "joints"—of life with this in mind. I thank God for the discernments, distinctions, and definitions made possible through the interior logic, the logos, or law-word, operating within me. I perceive the slow development of doctrine in the Church as a skeletal, life-supporting process, and I don't resent the "rigidity" of the clarity that results. I expect a continual supply of life-refreshing corpuscles to flow from within the rock-like stability that is bone, that is Church.

There is kinship between bare winter trees and my own hard, knobby, hard-working bones. They make so clear that living things are characterized as much by that which is hard, slow-changing, unyielding, and limited as by that which is flowing, daily renewed, malleable, and less distinct in form.

The skeleton is an arch—pelvis, foot—evenly distributing weight with a design I threaten to thwart if I impose my fears, my deformed mental model, my imbalanced force upon it. This leads me to the shape that architects say balances two types of force: the arch. Compression—the force that pushes down on you—is experienced as external circumstances, limitations, and demands. Tension—the discomfort of being pulled in opposite directions—is experienced as interior distress.

Weight on a bridge (or building, or body) pushes down. The underside of the bridge is in tension as the endpoints rise, pulling against one another until the plank snaps or the heavy object breaks through. End posts (or walls, or toes) push back, but greater weight can be borne if an arch directs the force directly down through them to the ground. Instead of resisting the outward push, they are evenly pushed straight down, and so the force works to maintain their position.

Tremendous weight + very thick load-bearers = support, but less open space. To open more space, open up the arch by external buttressing—direct more force into the supporting ground. I trust that

8 – Architecture of Freedom: Bones

the entirety of God's law frees and supports me spiritually as a skeleton does physically, and I am learning to maintain a "posture" toward God of trust and complete reliance.

For greater grace and freedom of movement, I must learn to rely on my skeleton to support me—relaxing muscles and ligaments that otherwise try to take over the work, exacting a price in tension, then pain. Bones speak to me of posture and poise. I do not need to clench and tighten my being to stay "upright" and "in good alignment"; rather, I must trust in the law that Christ fulfills within me. My freedom, my dynamic equilibrium, radiates outward from the very marrow of my being, where He is a fountain of refreshment and renewal.

Though it sounds a bit gruesome, the practice of distributing saints' bones appeals to my sensibilities! Some virtue of holiness seems, clearly, to reside in our physical and material relics, and bones last longer than all the rest. There is a story in Scripture of a dead man who was tossed in beside the holy prophet Elisha's bones and was thus brought miraculously back to life (2 Kings 13:21). It makes me wonder how my behavior, my acquisition of virtue, my adherence to God's laws might be affecting my bones, marrow, and blood.

The expansion of the interior dimension of persons is exactly what I picture when I say "spirituality," "capacity for Christ," "human freedom," or "inner spaciousness." There are opposite temptations made clearer by the contemplation of the arch. When you experience discomfort, you might tense up against it (thickening the walls, closing in on yourself, tightening in fear) or give way completely and disintegrate. Neither solution is a good one, because both ruin the balance between structure and space suggested by architectural ideals. In both cases, the interior dimension is reduced.

You need, rather, to learn to "open the arch" when interior discomfort demonstrates the need for greater accommodation of tensions and to "strengthen the supports" when exterior pressures threaten to crush you. Prayer, of course, helps in both directions. Prayer helps open and infuse you with light and grace to bear tensions. Prayer also helps strengthen resolution, virtue, and courage—structural elements that give you staying power and help force to be directed straight down into the Ground of Being, who can take anything.

I know there are things I won't realize about myself, about the spiritual life, without understanding bones more fully! One lifetime isn't enough to begin to plumb all these depths. Eternity will be anything but boring if the taste of wonder is any indication.

9 – Triune Form: Water

SOME PEOPLE worry that all "religious" symbols might be banned in our increasingly secular world. No problem, I say. If so, we still will possess the indications of God that fill Creation with His "fingerprints". The removal of crosses, statues, the fish symbol, or pictures of saints might inspire us to look around more for other windows into the Mystery. Like water. Take away my crucifix and I will sit down with a glass of water to contemplate the glory of God!

Start with its triune form: expressed as "gas," as "liquid," and as "solid ice". Water is the only substance where all three states can be readily observed in everyday life on earth. Water is the substance within which we live—our atmosphere—and which moves within us. It makes up 71 percent of the earth's surface and 50 to 60 percent of the human body.

Fish in ponds appreciate the fact that water floats as it freezes, instead of sinking—leaving them free to overwinter below. This reminds me of Christ's "burden that is light"—the form that does not oppress but that protects my freedom.

Look at the water within the body. It is as crucial a substance as grace is for the soul. I can get "dehydrated" spiritually, too. Just as physical dehydration is not perceived until after the body's self-defense mechanisms have begun to react (at some cost to the organism as a whole), I can be "shutting down" or experiencing "inflammation" before I realize my need for the refreshment of God's grace. I need to partake consciously of the abundant means of grace, not wait for a crisis that drives me to Him parched and injured.

Speaking of abundance, is there any greater symbol for "life abundant" than water? God keeps on raining down blessings and mercy on the just and unjust alike, providing water even for the barren desert through His Church and His people. Each of us is a little vessel, or channel of grace. We are here—you are here—to give the cup of water in His name, and to make the desert flower, so abundant is the supply.

The washing of the water of the Word—Scripture's cleansing power—reminds me of the lymph: white warrior blood cells in water, defending me and carrying off the enemy! This connects to the bones, which are factories for blood cells. At the deepest level of your physical being, then, law is intimately connected with grace. How often the words of God have strengthened me and renewed my soul, like a cup of refreshing water. Washing is an essential symbol of Christ's servant leadership and of the priestly humility by which we are served through His pope and priests. His blood continues to wash our bodies, and we float within the sea of His divine mercy—symbolized (of course!) by the water that flowed from His side. This water, mingled with blood, is also a maternal, child-birthing image. When you see water, do you think, "Jesus, I trust in You"?

Water also turns my thoughts to Mary, so full of grace, so pure, so transparent, so humbly available to all of us who take her for granted. Water is called the "universal solvent"—in time it manages to wear down all resistance. This, too, reminds me of our Blessed Mother's graceful, water-like patience. Naturally, she also had her origin "within the bones" of Israel's Law.

When water is blown and tossed about in the upper atmosphere, the most beautiful crystals are formed. Linked together in forms that speak of sacred order, holy geometry, peace in chaos, water molecules form a sort of "community." Two water molecules will bounce away from one another without some particle to settle them together. They need a little something to help them bond, at first, just as any two of us bond better over a shared book, a service project, or a common interest. That tiny seed of two together has enough staying power to provide the basis for the formation of snowflakes. It reminds me that, wherever two or more are gathered, and committed to unity, Jesus in the midst begins to create true community. I don't need to find a crowd but just one other to bond with in His name. He'll do the rest.

The healing science of homeopathy is based on water's capacity to receive the vibrational "signature" of substances within it. Somehow, the need of the body is met by the water-borne information in the

9 – Triune Form: Water

medicine. Like noise-cancelling headphones that work by meeting sound with dampening sound, these remedies restore equilibrium. Modern oscilloscopes have confirmed what homeopathic healers knew "in their bones," in their beings—that water is a messenger of healing, communicating with even unspoken cries for help. How like the Holy Spirit!

Water for cleansing, water troubled by an angel for healing, water for pure delight, water leaving minerals deposited as opals, water suddenly causing catastrophic change, water ever-so-slowly smoothing the rough surface, water as light's reflecting pool and sound's resonant substance, miraculous water from a desert rock and from the side of Christ, water moving continually through its cycle like the flow of love meeting need, water as the spring of civilizations, water organized as unrepeatable snowflake forms, water as home to glorious creatures, water mediated through materials as wine, water as a trinitarian bond of atoms (two hydrogens, one oxygen)—my mind is overwhelmed, humbled, and delighted by it all.

Water—the wonder of the world, if only the world would wonder! May some drop of all this water plunge you into the ocean of mercy as you look through its magnifying lens.

10 – Windows Through Words: Poetry

I teach a class in poetry called "Seeing through Words." I love words and delight in playing with them, sharing them, discovering them, and using them to craft poems. I want others to love words, primarily because the Word is God and has ordered our very being to the use of words. Without them, without the power to receive meaning through them and represent reality with them, we are less whole, less fully who we are meant to be.

Words convey imagery—they correspond to the power of the imagination, or the inner seeing that is foundational for stories but also for memory, empathy, vision, and creativity. Words convey meaning—they correspond to the power of the intellect, or the mental understanding that is crucial for conversation, confession, evangelization, and every act of resistance to tyranny. Words create dimension—they correspond to the delight and depth of the human soul and are the support for its growth in the capacity to apprehend reality.

The wholeness of form is re-presented to the mind through the senses. The more complete the re-presentation, the more the form can touch the heart, can affect us, can be apprehended whole-ly. Imagination and technology can generate nonreal forms that excite, please, distract, and engage attention. But unless we do the work of *realizing* these forms, or of seeing through them to what is real, these nonforms reduce our ability to take in what is real. Disconnection from reality is dangerous. Poetry helps us reconnect with words, and with our senses, and with our own interior capacity to know in a whole way.

Poetry, as a nonpractical form honoring words in all their glory, is meant to be heard. Oral-aural experience touches our hearts in a way that merely seeing words on a page cannot. Recovering the capacity to enjoy poetry can be hard work if we have lost patience for savoring words, or lost capacity for hearing or for being affected.

10 – Windows Through Words: Poetry

It's important to realize that this is work worth doing if we want to expand the "inner spaciousness" of our own souls.

My mantra is, "Look through, not at!" Unless you learn to look through reality, representations, and words to deeper meaning, to transcendent values, to your own destiny, you are in danger of mistaking your own sight for objective truth. We are to walk by faith, and not by sight, for this reason: our sight is so easily misled, flattened into mistaking accidents for essences and parts for wholes. True seeing is a capacity of the soul. Poetry helps you develop the kind of in-sight that combines head and heart into a vessel for the work of the Spirit, who gives genuine understanding.

Through words you can discuss what *is* (concrete details, actuality), what *is not* (memory, idea, abstraction, future), and what *both is and is not* (juxtaposition, paradox, tension). Poetry gets much of its power from this third kind of word work. The capacity to see one thing *by means of* another, to juxtapose unconnected things and find proportion and links between them, to handle the often paradoxical nature of reality or the seemingly untenable contradictions of life—this is the capacity of the human soul for being a vessel for the Holy Spirit.

At the very least, poetry trains us to think metaphorically and to see in real things (like bones, bridges, trees, oceans) metaphors that expand our understanding of other realities and deepen our spiritual life. Science, religion, dialogue, education depend hugely on the capacity to draw meaning from metaphors and to learn "slantwise" by seeing the unfamiliar beside what we already understand.

To be a person who can see through words, you need passion. The heart must be able to be affected. Poetry and music help us make powerful emotions manageable. By bringing experience down to a size we can apprehend (not control!) and into a form with clear boundaries, poems help us make our way through intense emotions that could overwhelm us, like a flooded river overflowing its banks. They also link our emotions to the common experience of mankind and help us develop empathy for others.

11 – Transforming the World: Trees

I LOVE TO THINK about trees! Psalm 1 tells me that, somehow, persons are "like trees," and that piques my interest. As object lessons for spiritual seekers, few things are as rich in associations. Can you picture yourself as a tree? Where are you planted? How deep and wide are your roots spread? Who shelters in your branches? Are you evergreen or deciduous? What kind of fruit do you (or will you) bear?

Trees have the capacity to take in nonliving minerals from the earth and transform them into the life-giving materials of sap, leaf, and fruit. When I think of people living in subhuman conditions, this reminds me that there are still wondrous and hopeful possibilities for them. Where there is a human person—even if he is weak, beaten down, poor—there is potential for transformation and the flow of grace into the world.

Trees reach for the sun—turning constantly, as they grow, to face the light. They experience spiral growth that results in a greater capacity to bear weight than a purely vertical growth could give. Architects have learned from trees how to improve the load-bearing capacity of columns and other structures. This image changed the way I perceived my own "growing around in circles." I realized, through trees, that the many times I found myself going around again in old patterns, I was actually growing up, and growing stronger along the way.

The depth and spread of a tree's roots anchor it for the corresponding spread of its branches. There is an unseen symmetry, or balance, operating here that must also operate in your own growth. Tree branches push out against gravity according to the strength of this connection with the ground of being. Impatient as I've been to move up, move forward, trees have taught me to wait for the seasons to extend my deep anchor in place, in family, in the interior life, in the health of my body. I'm stronger when I don't extend outward, onward, upward past my core strength.

11 – Transforming the World: Trees

Trees in adverse conditions show amazing pluck and perseverance—sending out deep taproots, if necessary, into faraway underground springs of water. The psalmist tells us we will be "like trees planted by streams of water," but even those who seem distant are probably holding on for dear life to that hidden stream we take for granted – the "living water" of God's grace. At one point in my spiritual growth, tree study showed me a mistake I was making. I'd been trying to achieve an equilibrium that was immovable, firm, unbending. Of course trees do grow huge and mighty, but the ones I needed to wonder at in those days were the saplings. Their strength-in-yielding to the pressure of wind gave me a metaphor for a dynamic balance that could spring back, dance in storms, bend. Trees are poised, but not rigid. Even giant redwoods are responsive to the movement of wind; still turn to face the sun daily; still move toward water in the depths below. The combination of increasingly firm exterior with ever-renewing interior as a tree matures, takes over a larger territory, and becomes fruitful is instructive for you as you draw your life's boundaries.

J.R.R. Tolkien's portrayal of ancient trees as heroes doesn't surprise me. All around, trees stand like guardians, buffering my home from the wind. They purify the air I breathe, removing toxins from the polluted world and returning sweet oxygen without complaint. They seem to bear scarring and deformation with noble patience. If only I could follow their example more consistently!

Observation of trees as self-contained "fruit factories" led engineers to redesign real factories along greener, saner, more circular and beautiful lines. It's no surprise that the human beings in these new facilities feel more whole, more comfortable, and less at odds with their own humanity. One quality they noticed was the overabundant productivity of trees. The seeming wastes of "production" (all those excess apples on the ground) were neatly recycled right back into nourishment for the tree itself. Their newly designed workplaces not only are more full of light and air, more hospitable to the workers, and more committed to the careful handling of toxins but also are elegant systems for recapturing and recycling the results of manufacture. I'm not the only one inspired by trees!

I can't think of trees without marveling at the process of grafting.

It may seem ordinary to orchard managers, but to me it seems miraculous that a cutting from one kind of tree could be spliced inseparably into another kind so as to create one tree with the strengths of both. I'm blessed to be "grafted in" to the Old Testament stock of the Jews—my flowering fruitfulness, as a Christian, deeply dependent upon the Law, the memory of God's promises, and the people formed by Sabbath-keeping. Marriage is a bit like this union, too, in its making two complementary persons into one.

Bare winter trees remind me of the body's bones, and of sentence diagrams—articulated structures supporting life and meaning. I love the way their branches seem to yearn upward, to clutch pieces of the sky. At the center of my being is a tree-like, three-dimensional yearning: toward the sun, toward water, toward fruit-giving in the world around me. In winter I look at those skeletons inked against watercolor dawns and sunsets and rejoice that God has made me to be like a tree.

A tree fills space fractally. Over and over, its characteristic geometry repeats as smaller and smaller limbs in every direction, until that shape can be seen from a distance, etched against the sky. This speaks to me of authenticity in organic growth, spiritual growth. What is essentially "me" will characterize the ultimate realization of "me" by reaching in every direction toward light. Though my final "form" will be very different from the look of infancy, it will be an expansion, an unfoldment rather than a negation of me. Jesus makes me more and more fully my own self every day—in Him I have realization of my own being.

TENSIONS
Workouts for Mind and Soul

Proposed: That the glory of man is to be free. This freedom is realized as he, amid the struggles of existence, exercises his power to wield himself according to his own desire and yield himself according to the desire of God. The hope, or end, of education is the free human person who brings glory to God through being himself.

These essays explore areas of tension, of polarity, in our thinking about human formation and freedom. Back and forth, the themes of wielding-and-yielding are woven through the warp threads held in tension, to help you form a picture of the "glorious freedom of the children of God." I've threaded the loom, and as you read and respond to these reflections, *you* are the weaver. No two readers will create the same fabric from these materials.

Notes on Growing Up – Work:
The Way of Youth and the Second Dimension of Freedom

Work—expending energy consciously to accomplish a particular purpose—is the second dimension of freedom. If wonder is a balanced stillness, poised before the whole of mystery framed by some particular reality, then work is a balance in tension, poised between realities, that engages the power of a person to move toward resolution. A hyper-child approach avoids work, words, discomfort, structure, formality—seeking in ease, fun, or pleasure a false leisure that debilitates the soul. A hyper-adult approach so identifies a person with his end products as to violate the soul by ignoring its higher-order needs for true leisure, transcendent meaning, and freedom of will.

Your response to God's authority is a function of your capacity to internalize authority itself. Where the "child" merely (and rightly) submits, the "youth" wrestles with external authority. Rebellion is not necessary for the individuation of human beings from their parents, but engagement is. It is a struggle to establish the rule of law over those aspects of self that resist its demands. Internal structures are freeing, whereas external ones eventually become prisons.

In any area of human accomplishment, a virtuoso is one with freedom, capacity, power, and skill. The capacity for work is cultivated by work—intellectual, physical, spiritual struggle to understand arguments, develop skills, resolve paradoxes, grow in virtue. It is strengthened by every free act of obedience, of service, of confession and reconciliation, of resistance to peer pressure or media manipulation, of perseverance through trials, of patience with your own weakness, of spiritual reading, of putting ideas into words, of fasting, of formal prayer, of response to a book or an invitation, of transforming materials creatively, or of cleaning up a mess.

You spend most of your life in the tension of "work." The more you appropriate the deep effects of work upon your soul, the more it becomes the means to your liberation. Children of God are, thus, freed from enslavement to work as an end in itself. If you wait until "playtime" for "spiritual things," you'll miss the engagement with work that is practically a fountain of youth.

12 – Education vs. Formation

Formed by the Potter?

GOD PROMISES to work in you, helping you both "to will and to do according to His purpose." Clearly, the formation of your soul is His gift to you—accomplished by the presence of Christ within your very being. His Holy Spirit vivifies your natural talents, desires, strengths, and circumstances—weaving "all things together for your good," to prepare you for eternal life with Him. He completes what He starts in you, knows you better than you know yourself, knits you together following His own design, and shapes you, as a potter shapes clay, into a pleasing vessel.

"Formation" is a word that implies a certain passivity in the material being formed. The shaped emptiness crafted on a potter's wheel calls to mind God's beautifully balanced application of interior and exterior pressure. A soul formed by the action of grace should grow more beautiful over time. Yet defects in both the "material" and the "fools" that God works with introduce an element of doubt as to the outcome. Even if your formation is God's own art project, you aren't entirely sure how well it will turn out! You realize, with trepidation, that you must cooperate in your own formation.

Tempting as it is to think of formation as a deeply private matter between the soul and her Lord, you cannot deny the impact of many variables of environment and influence—every one of which has as much potential to deform as to form her. Any attempt to participate in your own formation seems presumptuous, yet you react and respond to all that affects you, and you thus help to shape yourself for better or for worse. When you lead others, you wonder if your efforts can actually be formative. As a third party to the transaction, can you help form souls?

Souls at Work

Educated by Experts?

Perhaps what you really do for others is "educate." This word reminds us of the way parents, teachers, and books influence students externally. The educative process is usually handled by trained professionals. To take responsibility for your own education seems a bit uppity in its own way—equating yourself with experts. No one could expect you to give yourself what you don't have, so God surely doesn't intend for you to bootstrap your way into heaven. Yet yearbooks are full of kids voted "most likely to succeed" because they worked harder at doing well in school. Whose responsibility *is* education?

You might not give this much thought when the education at stake is calculus or world history, but when your soul is at stake, you need an answer. One way of looking at this is to consider spiritual education as the training you receive in theology, apologetics, doctrine, and Gregorian chant. Then you seek out the best teachers (for yourself or your children) and relax. With God working the formation from the inside, and good material pouring in, how can you go wrong? The only problem is, you've just sidelined your soul entirely, leaving your *self* (the "acting person," as Pope John Paul II called you) only a passive role in formation.

Let's try again. Could it be that God and teachers can only have their way with someone to the extent that he allows? Now the *person* is squarely in the driver's seat. You achieve your education, and your effort makes all the difference. The teacher's expertise is a resource you draw on in order to learn. You really are educating yourself. Plug those answers into the formation equation, though, and you have a person using God as a resource to get the needs of his soul met. Somehow a warning bell sounds. So far, we've seen two common solutions tried and found wanting in resolving the education/formation paradox.

Muddy Waters

So, we want to connect the two concepts, but when we try, our view of one muddies our thinking about the other.

12 – Education vs. Formation

You need a way of thinking about spiritual growth that includes your cooperation with the action of grace, your active receptivity to instruction, and the value of excellent teachers and orthodox doctrine. You know you aren't the agent of your own salvation, and you also know hard work actually helps you accomplish great things. You need a way of understanding your responsibility for your own becoming, without negating God's power and His desire to act upon your soul. You've got to be able to account for the action of environmental factors beyond a person's control, if you are the shaper of an environment where others are growing.

If you don't struggle with this paradox at all, you've likely let someone else do the thinking for you. If you leave your spiritual growth completely up to good religion teachers and God, you may barely notice as your soul stagnates or shrinks like a grape left too long on the vine. If you take charge of your development, trying hard to snatch the gold ring of holiness and get the biggest heavenly mansion or the most jewels in your crown, you may be unpleasantly surprised when your progress is thwarted at every turn. Can this be resolved?

How much can you "let go and let God"? Does holiness require years of study and intellectual application, or is it a free gift to all who love God and keep His commands? Could it be "enough" to receive the sacraments regularly and leave the effects on your soul up to God's action? Can't He get your soul formed without your participation? Or, *can* He with your interference? What effect does your environment have on your soul's shape? How much are you damaged by the way you've been formed, taught, raised, and influenced? Can the deformation be reversed, or healed?

You must "work out your salvation with fear and trembling." It is awe-full to realize you have been given power to affect an immortal soul! No one steps carelessly on such holy ground. It should be uncomfortable and challenging to consider these questions. The work of struggling with tensions like this is your active participation in your soul's formation. As you become conscious of the answers implicit in the formative and educative processes that have impacted you so far, you will engage your soul—mind, emotions, and will—in active cooperation with the work of the Spirit. This is what it takes to become free!

Who prepares your soul to enter heaven? Are people "taught" or "molded," or both? Who is doing that work? The person himself? God? Teachers? Parents? Society? Media? Does the education of the intellect affect the soul? Is religious education the one subject that involves mind and soul? If you are a factor in the "success" of your own education, how does the formation of your soul affect your capacity to learn skills and subjects?

You Write This Book

You have received an "education." You've been to school; parents and books have taught you; you've learned on the job; your interests have drawn you to seek instruction. What did that education have to do with the formation of your soul? Was it religious or secular? Was the environment hostile or collegial? Were you a passive-resistant or a willing-eager learner? Where was the locus of control—who called the shots? How has your formal education affected the way you approach spiritual development? Is your spiritual life characterized by looking for teachers, directors, good classes, a scope and sequence for progress?

You've had "formation." You can feel the way people and events have shaped you inwardly. You sense the impact of certain unmet needs, unfulfilled longings, and pains on your soul. You realize what a debt you owe to others for the love and faithfulness that surrounded you. Your soul has arrived at where it is almost unconsciously, so it may feel awkward to examine these factors and their formative effects. Your expectation for ongoing spiritual growth is related to all that has formed you so far. Are you finding it hard to trust that any good will come without constant effort? Are you seeking a return to the idyllic life of childhood, when faith came so effortlessly?

I want to help you stop thinking of education and formation as two unrelated spheres of life—the former external/intellectual and the latter internal/spiritual. Given that there is one person—you—being educated/formed and that your involvement in the process has a lot to do with the results, I want you to examine your own educative/formative process so far. This is not a time for judgment,

12 – Education vs. Formation

only for observation—for opening your eyes to the fact that the nature of your education/formation and the nature of your response to it have a bearing on the state of your soul today. Here, you begin a self-portrait, informed by a loving gaze, that includes, as much as is possible, the entirety of your education/formation history.

13 – Child vs. Adult

Be Like a Child

SCRIPTURE TELLS YOU to become like a little child, or risk missing out on the kingdom of heaven. You need to study childhood to know what God thinks will prepare you for eternity. As you grow up, you'll continually walk the way of the child in your relationship with God, the Father. That "way" is the way of wonder, of simplicity, of trust. Your work—the struggle or tension exposed here—is to retain and enlarge these qualities within the increasingly fast-paced, complex, and threatening world of adulthood.

Speed fights against wonder. Have you walked with a toddler? It takes patience to stop with him as he encounters the world, wondering, interested, amazed. Your desire to go faster is in tension with his desire to attend to everything he sees. If you learn from his example, you'll stop more often, go slower whenever you possibly can, look long and lovingly at everything that is. You need to drink in the world you've been speeding past. Your soul expands when your gaze opens. Speed flattens and contracts, deforming your being. Follow the child back to the capacity for delight.

Be simple! Oh, if it were that easy! For a child, it is, because he doesn't try to hold the past and its burdens in his mind, or the imagined future with its scenarios and stress. He simply is *here*, *now*, and you can learn that lesson from him. It's really a lesson in trust. The child can trust in mere, mortal parents, so shouldn't you be able to develop trust in the omnipotent Father? The child teaches the constant turning back to the parent, to the basics of life: comfort, shelter, safety, sustenance. Continual conversion—turning—will bring us home, too.

Grow Up in All Things

Is it unimportant, then, to do the work of growing up, to shoulder its duties manfully and provide for all the children and others who

13 – Child vs. Adult

cannot bear the weight? Scripture, after all, also tells us to "grow up in all things" and "put away childish things." If everyone remains in this blissful childhood, who's going to get the world's work done? It's a fine thing to hold up a state we can't stay in as an eternal condition! What do we gain by putting away childish things to become adults? There's definitely some tension here, and it comes from the false sense that maturation is a *narrowing*.

Granted, the adult bears a great deal for others and gives up much of childhood's vagueness in the process. You do feel your options narrowing, your choices constricting the range of future possibilities as you grow older. The adult who narrows to a pinpoint of self, however, is not being "responsible" but actually is becoming less "able-to-respond." In order to grow up without violating yourself, you must understand what Christ wants. In God's economy, to grow up is to grow more and more free. To do this, you must grow more able to take and hold the territory of your own soul.

To grow up is a glorious thing when it corresponds to growth in interior freedom! In true adulthood, there is no lack of adventure. The way of maturity is the way *through* work, struggle, and tension *to* the promised land. By responding to and acting on whatever you encounter, you grow in true response-ability. The child knows reality passively, with a poetic, un–self-conscious openness. You may go so much further. You have the capacity to go deeper, to know in words, to possess reality more fully through study. You take and hold territory open—both possessing the land, and dwelling in it richly–as you grow.

So, Which Is It?

In a world dominated by the factory-as-creator, you tend to think of things moving in a straight line from raw material to finished product. This colors your understanding of adulthood. You are frustrated when you get "called back" to childhood, as though you were being sent back to first grade. You chafe at the way of the child. Oddly, you may, simultaneously, be affected by the fantasy that grown-ups get to do whatever they want. You may chafe at the way of the adult when it calls for fighting giants, relinquishment, and hard work.

You could end up completely paralyzed! Fortunately, God meets you right where you are and pulls you through. If you're happily engaged in the here and now, He quickens your curiosity, your desire to know more, to dig deeper into things, to work to understand more fully. If your heart is affected by someone's pain, you have the freedom and maturity to respond in adult solidarity to restore justice. A child would have to take his sadness to an adult for help, but your more mature reason and intelligence enable truly free action—the engagement of your will. With each free act, your freedom grows.

Unlike adults who forget how to be also like needy children, you needn't ever feel you must bear your trials alone. While they stoically increase in self-defense against pain, you will be bearing suffering like a child, in the arms of your loving Father. Those without hope face death as the final contraction. You will face it as the final expansion of a soul that steadily grew more and more spacious and free as you grew up. Who would *not* want the delights of spiritual maturation, if they only knew about them? This is the best kept secret in the never-never land of modern perpetual childhood!

If childhood is the stage of natural, poetic encounter with the beauty of Creation, adulthood is the stage of richly crafted, poetic representation of that encounter. Certainly, one reason your soul's enemy fights against your maturation is that the adult is a fruitful being, a multiplier of reality, truth, and beauty, a creative power he would prefer to crush into infantile impotence. The world teaches you that to grow up is either to relinquish the joys of childhood or to debase yourself by holding on to the ways of infants. God teaches you that growing up frees you to fully possess the gifts of the child, *and* to follow the way of the child into heaven.

14 – Work vs. Leisure

You've Got Work to Do

GOD CREATED YOU "for good works, which He has prepared for you to do" (Ephesians 2:10). The work you do, the things you create, are central features of your life. In a sense, your work *is* you, is your mark on the world, or your legacy. If your vocation and the daily work you do to support yourself and your loved ones are the same, you probably have a sense of great satisfaction. If not, you might experience frustration, or a sense that work is getting in the way of your highest calling. Work both expresses and affects your interior, spiritual life.

Adam was called to work not as a punishment for sin[1] but as the means to his realization of himself and of the created world. Only when, through Adam's fall, nature lost its rightly-ordered "husbandman" did it begin to fight against him and to groan in expectation of his restoration in Christ. If work has become onerous for you, it is crucial that you find some way to honor and protect your essential human, interior freedom. Unless you can freely choose even what seems imposed on you, the time of bondage will be debilitating. When the Israelites were delivered from slavery, for example, they needed forty more years of wandering in the desert to "man up" and become capable of entering into their rightful destiny.[2]

---

1. Expulsion from Eden, as punishment for sin, also involved the newly-burdensome nature of work in a fallen world. "God places him in the garden. There he lives 'to till and keep it.' Work is not yet a burden, but rather the collaboration of man and woman with God in perfecting the visible creation." (*Catechism of the Catholic Church*, 378)

2. The murmuring of the Israelites against God's plan to move them into the Promised Land resulted in a punishment (forty years more wandering) that would help them mature as a people. Though one generation would die, their children would grow capable of entering that land freely. See Numbers 14 for the story.

How much investment do you need to make in yourself in order to do your work? You spend time learning and practicing skills; you need continuing education or constant reading to keep up in your field. You may need advanced credentials, extra calories to fuel physical labor, expensive art supplies, or pricey professional memberships to stay on your game. The ongoing flow of resources into the "me" reservoir seems natural and inevitable to you. Yet, there is a danger in all this. The more you identify with the work you do, the more likely you are to misunderstand the idea of leisure.

The Weekend—Get Over It

In our secularized culture, we've gone overboard linking man to the work he performs. Man's reason for being is, for much of society, the productivity he provides or the economic value he adds to the GNP. In this culture of man-the-worker, rest is just another resource invested to make a better worker. Blessed Pope John Paul II warned us against the "weekend" mentality—the equation of rest with periodic machine downtime, in which non-work is the highest value instead of true restoration of the person. Human beings, he said, must be rested in ways that correspond to being, not to producing.

The first need of the soul is holy leisure: Sabbath rest, centered in the Eucharist, that corresponds to your relationship with God as the bearer of His image. That image rests on your very *being* and is ordered to eternal life in heaven, not to life on the job. No matter how satisfying your work is, the weekly reminder that you have value that transcends that work puts it into proper perspective. Without that perspective, you are prey to those who would make you a mechanical component of a never-stopping materialism factory, which uses its "human resources" up and spits them out with no regard for humanity or dignity.

Wait, didn't I just say God made you for the work He called you to do? Shouldn't you be willing to spend yourself completely for, and be used up for, your work, if necessary? Well, there's one problem with this theory. God Himself commanded the rest, the holy Sabbath. So He has weighed in, not *against* work, but *for* the human person. This leisure is not just another investment you make or

14 – Work vs. Leisure

price you pay in time for the privilege of working. It's not about you, in fact, at all. It's about God, and understanding it right-side up clarifies this distinction.

Holy leisure turns you right-side up and sets you free from the very dangerous mentality of the prevailing culture. To do the works God created you to do, you must do the work of your own becoming. All that other investment you've made is part of this, but one thing overshadows everything you do in order to accomplish you: the thing that God does! "It is He who works in you to will and to act according to His good purpose" (Philippians 2:13). He takes the "you" you offer to Him as a vessel and fills it with gifts that overflow in abundance to those around you. He encounters whomever you meet and invites them to Himself.

Leisure—The Basis of Real Work

The tension we are working with here is not the balance between action and contemplation. Holy leisure exposes the difference between the way we get work done and the way God does. Your daily work, whether it is drudgery that barely sustains life, volunteer humanitarian work, or highly paid and influential expertise is important for its effects upon your soul and for whatever good it does for others. But it pales in comparison to the work He does through you in the world when you are most truly and fully yourself. That wholeness and authenticity of your being is served by true leisure.

It may frustrate you to hear that whatever you spend most of your time and resources doing, is not actually the aspect of your being that gets the payoff of results for God's kingdom. We are trained to think of cost-benefit tradeoffs and time-and-motion efficiency. This revelation sort of offends a deep sense of fairness. That God can do more in this world through one day of your holy inaction than through all your hard work seems counterintuitive. That's because your intuition hasn't been trained yet by holy leisure! But hold on…

It is not as though those other days don't matter at all. Your efforts have their place in God's economy. That place just isn't as big as you thought, and the Sabbath is so much bigger, it seems to dwarf those other days. To the extent you discover holy leisure, you'll notice God getting you done by your work as much as your work getting done by you. Whatever issues you struggle with during your workday become opportunities for Him to educate your soul in freedom. More and more, the external and internal work being done comes into better integration.

Like a lock whose tumblers click into alignment and open, your soul opens in a new way when your daily work is suffused with true leisure. This rest doesn't make you unfit for work; rather, it keeps you from valuing fitness-for-work over greater things. Your "fitness" for eternity—your capacity to feast and celebrate and give glory to God—is of immensely great value to God because it prepares your soul for communion with Him. You are more important to Him than anything you can accomplish, yet He justly values those works of yours. The formation of your soul depends on the eucharistic Sabbath as on no other single practice.

The struggle inherent in this tension is to work out how you will best honor the commandment to keep the Sabbath holy in a way that restores your own wholeness.

15 – Freedom vs. Form

Freedom is Exhilarating

HAVE you struggled to learn to play the piano? To run track? To write poetry? To paint or sculpt? To learn French? Then you've been introduced to the tension between form and freedom. We don't tend to think of spiritual growth as a "skill set" you can learn, but the movement from "beginner" to "master" or "convert" to "saint" follows a similar trajectory of learning-by-doing. Discipline, or form, is the means by which freedom is realized, in whatever arena sets the stage for your struggle. Your ideas about what that freedom will look like in the spiritual realm affect your progress.

As a person, you belong to yourself and can act to exercise the free will God gave you. True, you belong to Him, but you have dominion over yourself—the ability to give yourself magnanimously, to maintain your human virtues, to give your word as a promise, to judge for yourself what action to take, to follow your own desires, to design your own Sabbath practices, to invest yourself in the world and its affairs, to correct injustice, to suffer creatively, to cultivate relationships, to speak the truth in love, and more! But, do you want to be this free?

It's a bit scary, all this free agency of yours! What if you choose the wrong action? Judge on the basis of incomplete information? Pursue something that leads you astray from the narrow way God wants you to follow? What if your freedom leads you into license, your untrained conscience into sin, or your disordered desire into the bondage of addiction? Suddenly, freedom seems less appealing. Christ may have come to set you free, but how in the world does He expect you to *get* full freedom without running all these risks? It's a relief to return to form!

Souls at Work

Form is Freeing

"Form" is the safe haven from the dangers of unrestrained freedom. Like the banks of a river or the protection of parental supervision, form constrains and directs as it trains you in freedom. In the case of spiritual freedom, you are boundaried by the clear doctrines of the Church. You needn't worry about falling for destructive ideas if you stay in those bounds. The "form" of holy obligations like Mass attendance, regular confession, and fasting helps you develop the strength of character that will keep your feet on the narrow way. Formal prayer gives you a pattern to follow confidently.

The external authority of law can certainly keep you from doing whatever you want, but in that way it helps protect you from your own worst potential. Just how free can you be if you are bound by laws, rules, rites, and duties? When those constraints go too far, aren't you supposed to fight against them? If you give in docilely to whoever tells you what to do, how do you develop your own ability to exercise free agency? Surely those rites and duties can become so empty of meaning that they have no value in teaching you virtue or responsibility.

Yes, you need to learn to read music, but also to play with freedom and delight. Yes, you must endure the discipline of ball-handling drills, but when do you get to play the real game? You're willing to be disciplined, but it would help to understand what the results will be. What does spiritual, or interior, "freedom" mean, and what forms, what drills, what disciplines get you there? Is freedom possible for you if you aren't yet a saint? Who can help you assess your progress?

Freedom is Hard Work

The process of finding freedom through form involves real work, real discomfort, real danger. On the one hand, you must exercise freedom to grow in freedom. Your efforts will be imperfect, landing you in the scary zone occupied by lawless, rebellious people who scoff at Truth and mistake license for liberty. On the other hand, you must stay within certain bounds, obey laws, and remain in Christ and His Church in order to become free. You'll be tempted to snug-

15 – Freedom vs. Form

gle up in the security of a program of behavioral legalism that never becomes the true, internal law directing your actions from within.

Becoming fully free can be compared with becoming fully mature. The only way to escape this is to sell yourself into slavery or remain in the relative impotence of infancy. If you raise children, you must struggle with this tension on their behalf. Not everyone is called to become an athletic superstar, a prima ballerina, or a concert pianist. As human beings made new in Christ, however, you are called to the glorious freedom of the children of God.

You may be physically paralyzed or even in prison and still learn to be inwardly, spiritually free. Political freedom may be worth fighting for, and freedom from injustice worth dying for. How much more is the freedom to *be* fully human, fully yourself, worth working for? If you want to *run* in the path of God's commands, be holy, attract people to His Church, or fulfill your vocation, you must enter into the struggle between form and freedom.

It takes work to internalize the laws signified by the Church's rites, requirements, forms, and gestures. The work you do will make it easier to hand on those forms to your children. Instead of chafing at the responses, obligations, and traditions, embrace them. Society teaches that form is a restriction on freedom. God teaches that freedom comes *through* form.

16 – Art vs. Intellect

I'm No Intellectual

You've noticed that some extremely intelligent people don't believe in God. How reliable can "intellect" be if its very strength allows for such patent weakness? You are right to suspect that your belief in Truth springs not only from your intellectual ability to understand and assent to that Truth but also from your willingness to obey it. Why bother, then, unless your career requires it, to work at developing intellectual faculties—the power of your mind to remember, learn, imagine, and judge? Plenty of saints couldn't even read, and the Word of God is proclaimed orally every Sunday.

There are many models for thinking about how your mind works and for increasing your intellectual strengths. There are various types of intelligence, and few people are equally strong in them all. Your question is, How much should *you* struggle to overcome intellectual weakness in order to love God "with your whole mind," as Scripture teaches? Yours is not an academic interest in the fine points of metacognition, but an active need to decide how to invest your time and what goals to set for building your own mind's "wholeness" without compromising your ability to believe true doctrines and obey them.

You don't want to sell your soul for a display of framed credentials, but you hear that God wants you "transformed by the renewing of your mind." You know you could get more out of spiritual reading and catechism classes if you had more mental muscle or more theology training, but obviously you've got to stand on the shoulders of giants like St. Augustine and Pope Benedict XVI, no matter how high your own IQ. Thank God for them, and for all the champions whose intellectual prowess assists lesser mortals in simplified, accessible theological explanations.

16 – Art vs. Intellect

But I'm No Artist, Either

What you really need is to live out the things you already know! You may be far from *real*-izing in practice what your mind has already received as theological theories. When you move from "knowing" to "doing," you see that spiritual growth involves art—consciously putting ideas into practice. Perhaps *this* is where you should invest more time. Artists have latitude to be more concrete, more practical than "intellectuals." Far from the ivory towers, artists seem free from academia's hollow theories—more earthy, authentic, and animated. These are glad tidings to you if you want your spiritual life to stay real, grounded, in touch.

If you think of spiritual growth as "artistic," you get all this creative freedom in exchange for some new risks. Artists certainly aren't immune to the self-seeking, self-referential blindness of intellectuals. Their quest for "pure" art, in fact, leads to propaganda in much the same way that "pure" science, divorced from theology, led the intelligentsia to atheism after the Reformation. The interior light can be just as dark for an artist as for a scientist, or a professor of theology. Contrary to the romantic notion of the artist as somehow beyond law in the muse-inspired fog of semi-deity, the true artist is subject to laws, the constraints of reality, the rigors of study and practice, and the burdens of truth. Even if you are a spiritual "artist," you've got your work cut out for you!

You continually receive messages you must evaluate intelligently. Advertisements, news, editorials, political cartoons, paintings, music, and other people's lives (virtual, literary, real, or imagined) all present arguments you must respond to thoughtfully. They each demand a judgment and you comply (How freely? How well informed? How consciously?), whether you have good judgment and a well-formed conscience or not. Without the capacity to judge well, you risk having the world's thought manipulators make your choices for you. Without the capacity to respond creatively and artistically, to put your judgments into practice in the midst of a hostile culture, you risk growing impotent to change that culture.

What is the value of "faith" that gets doctrines wrong or falls easy prey to spurious reasoning and good-looking liars? Faith without works is dead, so there must be some way to balance your "knowing" and your "doing" effectively. The tension between sharpening your intellectual faculties and working on practical expressions of faith (to the extent you understand it) is not a war between you and the "world" or a tug-of-war between an "external" and an "internal" good, so it's less easy to resolve, perhaps. As a tension between two paths of practice—both valuable—this one requires a creative response from you that takes your own gifts and interests into account.

Whole Imagination

It would be much easier to choose one or the other—art or intellect—to practice, and that is what many people do, whether they choose consciously or not. This is better than ignoring them both, but less demanding than holding open the possibility of a resolution—that is, your unique response—crafted with understanding *and* creativity. The work of responding is the work of creating your own freedom. Freedom takes the shape, in this case, of imagination. How much capacity do you have to inhabit the territory of your own mind, and to *real*-ize what you envision there?

Your imagination, like your freedom, is a risky place. There are real dangers in this "promised land," but this rich and fertile territory is the birthright of human beings. You'll need to learn discipline of the imagination as it grows within you, but that's no reason to stay in the desert! The human imagination—cultivated by both intellectual *and* artistic disciplines—is a channel for grace to enter the world in creative new forms. As proof of its potential, notice how many elements of "worldly culture" fight against it. Truly, there are giants at the entrance to this abundant land.

Your senses, your memory, your capacity for poetic knowledge are besieged by media designed to turn individuals into masses of easily manipulated automatons. Your beliefs are assailed by lies, illogic, and irreverence on a daily basis. Your imagination is trained to respond to surface stimuli as popular culture flattens you into a cardboard cutout of a person. If you "go with the flow," you may lose all sense of self and the interior spaciousness of freedom that

16 – Art vs. Intellect

corresponds to a well-nourished and flourishing imaginative capacity. In your fight against this deadening of your mind, you need excellent stories, beautiful works of art, and superlative music to help protect your intellectual faculties from atrophy.

17 – Individual vs. Community

I've Got to Be Me

IN THE UNITED STATES, the individual is valued over the state. His liberties are supposed to be protected against the encroachment of fellow citizens and against suppression by the government. We tend to think of freedom as an attribute of individuals released from the authority of forms and hierarchical order. In the extreme, we pull against one another in a disintegrating way, but in general this pulling holds our self-interest in balance and in check. We revere the lone hero, the singular and self-made man or woman. We suspect the ulterior motives of anyone who would limit our freedom of self-will and self-determination.

Ironically, the near-complete takeover of "individual" by "corporate" America began with this same individualistic self-interest. The Industrial Revolution left the means of production in a few hands, and these new magnates felt entitled to "add lands to lands" in a cancerous takeover of the body politic. Where amalgamation has failed to negate the individual human person, atomization sweeps up. Persons bereft of faith, of place, of heritage, of a coherent sense of self wander in increasing numbers, like zombies, through a barren social landscape where only the strong seem to survive. Humanity, debased by a culture that all but worships self, has lost the human person.

The good news is the Catholic Church and its plot to recapitulate the human person! This book, for instance, was written in response to Blessed Pope John Paul's marching orders to that effect. The answer to the social woes we face and the principle of the coming of Christ's kingdom into this world are one and the same: the human person. Restored to his dignity and freedom by the power of the Holy Spirit, the Individual-with-a-capital-"I" is the place from which Christ Himself will voice a creative response to the realities "I" encounter.

17 – Individual vs. Community

Do Not Forsake the Fellowship

On the other hand, the human person was designed to need community. He cannot be fully realized outside the demands and even the impedances of life in community. We really do need one another. In times of crisis, on Make a Difference Day, and in thousands of volunteer organizations, you see the great community-mindedness of Americans. However separate we are, we seem to relish the opportunity to work together, at least for a while. It's not just liberals who care about the social fabric, the rearing of the village's children, and the safety of neighborhoods, for example.

We may have vastly different ideas about what constitutes our "social duty," who pays for common goods, what regulation of self is necessary to achieve some social parity. But most agree it is not just "me" that matters. We may actually agree so readily that we too easily subordinate self-interest to the ideal of the common good. If all tension is perceived as "bad," then we may rush to give up self whenever self-and-other seems to be a source of conflict. The damage this self-violation does to the social fabric is much less visible than, but no less real than, that done by individualistic self-seeking.

What we want, then, is the community of free, mature, virtuous persons who agree to do the work of harmonizing the interests of self and other, local and global community, primary and secondary loyalties. Opportunities to learn and practice this type of interaction are increasingly rare. No one seems to have the time it takes to get together, much less to dwell upon the philosophies and structures framing community life. So, we settle for approximations to life in community.

As Catholics, we're already aware that Christ saves us both personally and as a body—His body, the Church. We still face the practical tensions of how much time to spend with family and friends, whether to join associations, how to set boundaries around personal time and space while living with others, etc. As a question of our formation in freedom, though, the tension between self and self-incorporated takes on greater significance. Relationships involve constant constraints on our freedom, but we can't live without them. We need time alone for prayer, for conversation with

God, for spiritual growth, but if we haven't learned to be truly present to other people, we find it hard to be present to Christ.

Your Community Needs You

The Church, then, is the best hope for a training ground in community that supports the deep individuation and full realization of human persons. In its universality is the gravitas we need to anchor us as society flops back and forth from the extreme of individualism to that of communitarianism. Its doctrines are the center that will hold—the organizing principle for temperance of destructive self-will and cultivation of creative self-expression. In the particularity of local parishes, sodalities of every charism, and individual confession, we have support for the particularity of each person.

As ever, the Catholic Church is the via media between extremes that vie with one another for the lead role in the negation of the human person. She is both model and womb for the development of free man—the embodiment of God's own answer to the question, "Is the individual or the body more valuable?" By refusing to give an "either-or" response, she leads each one of us to the freedom of formulating his own, true, free response. Like a good teacher, she offers a choice where a prescription or proscription would get things done more efficiently.

In your struggle to answer the questions that arise from this tension, keep in mind that the easy answer is often the one that violates one or the other party in tension. If you do not face the discomfort of offering yourself in truth and in freedom to the communities you are building, you deprive them of the greatest gift: the free gift of self. Your family, your lay association, your parish—even your business corporation, political party, or civic choir—needs you to be you in order to thrive. The more fully realized you are, the more your communities and your individual personhood will prosper.

18 – Church vs. Culture

Don't Be Worldly

DO NOT BE CONFORMED to the pattern of this world. Be in the world, but not of it. It's pretty clear we Catholics are supposed to be a people set apart, noticeably different from the non-Catholics around us. If we're willing to be reviled and persecuted for the sake of Christ, we won't balk at sticking out a bit in the world we inhabit. For many Catholics, though, it's much easier to go "incognito"—blending in with the dominant social culture. Calling attention to yourself in a culture where sameness equals safety can be risky. Who wants to be a pariah?

Yet, even those who "go native" can seem, for all their fashion sense, media lore, and tech savvy, like foreigners to their neighbors. The strangeness of going to Mass instead of Starbucks on Sundays, declining to play in Sabbath ball games, wearing a smudge of ashes to work, or refusing to donate to Planned Parenthood are all but impossible for them to understand. If they see you at a pro-life rally, or notice your Lenten fast from Facebook, you are not going to seem "normal," however hard you try!

You may as well be different. At least secular culture glorifies the idea of being "original," though this usually results in a boring monotony of self-expressed groupthink. It's possible that, by embracing the cultural oddities of Catholic life, you will win, if not your neighbor's endorsement, at least his interest. The culture you create consists of the things you do and create when you are at leisure—just being you.

What does distinctively Catholic culture look like for you and your family? Conversely, how much does your family culture look and feel just like that of the pagan next door? As you express yourself, you can't follow a formula. You can't even guarantee that the signs you use to articulate who you are (your clothes, words, bumper stickers, T-shirt slogans, tag lines, eucharistic processions, etc.) will be understood by anyone the way you mean them. The business of "signifying yourself" occurs in the "youth" stage as you emerge from total identification with parents and then family, and as you broaden and expand "You" at any age. You'll have to look to Christ for your own, free responses and then try to help people understand what you mean by them. You are, potentially, an encounter with Christ for whoever "receives" the messages you send.

The Enemy Is Us

Sadly, many Catholics are as likely as people in the secular world to have premarital sex, abortions, porn addictions, substance abuse problems, or broken marriages. These are culturally conditioned behaviors, but you must be able to step away from the culture to see the forest despite the distraction of the trees. The roots of destructive behavior lie in cultural norms, media messages, music preferences, educational institutions and practices, peer pressure, manipulation by marketing experts, etc.

The forms we create and inhabit organize our values for communication to others, exerting pressure toward those values. When every space we inhabit is shaped by a culture of mediocrity, immorality, lawlessness, cynicism, materialism, and childish disrespect, we will be deformed, pressured toward a downward homogeneity, blinded to our own conformity with the patterns of this world.

Questioning your acceptance of cultural norms may make you feel like a judgmental spoilsport. If you love your fellow students, neighbors, and coworkers, you want to be like them, want to be seen as one of them, want them to feel your acceptance. How can you bless them if you're busy calling down fire on their abominations? How can you be light in the darkness if you're indistinguishable from them? What did St. Paul mean when he said, "I have become all things to all men, that I might save some"? How much good can we really do if we don't dwell in the same 'hoods, habits, and humor that "they" inhabit? Shouldn't we learn "their" language and metaphors—their music, movies, fads, and fashions?

18 – Church vs. Culture

How to Build a Bridge

Worse yet, all this "we" and "they" talk may be the real problem. Catholics are fundamentally like everyone else—just as needy, broken, and human. To speak of distinctions may prevent the empathic dialogue that builds bridges. You cannot have true compassion (literally, suffering with) until you have the humility to stoop right down to any level and share it with your fellow human being. But is this compassion, or codependent enabling? Can you raise anyone from the mire if you don't get up and out yourself? Perhaps it feels snobbish even to speak of "low" and "high" morals and behaviors.

So, what really matters? Essences or accidents? The interior things that are true about you, whether you express them or not, or the exterior means by which you communicate these truths? The things that set you apart from others, or the things that you have in common? Loving communication of truth is our great commission. Only a "both-and" response will suffice.

The signs by which you indicate who you are invite the judgment and response of whoever is near you. You really can't help expressing yourself (and thus, generating a "culture" of sorts), though you can mask and misrepresent yourself. The "truth" of your contributions to culture consists of the "truth" about you, and about Christ living within you. How much correspondence is there between your "essence" and your "accidents"? How free are you to *be* you, even if that means "different"? What if signs change meaning with the times?

You are stepping from the relative shelter of *being* into the turbulent public forum where your being is communicated to others in the context of a storm of other messages. You must be willing to "invest in failure" time and time again, as you try to give authentic witness to your values, desires, and beliefs in the midst of a "persecution" of misunderstanding and hostility.

19 – Safety vs. Risk

The Risk of Education

WHAT IS THE ROLE of risk-taking in your formation? My favorite learning laboratory for this tension is driver's education. As I supervise my teen's first driving experiences, I learn more and more about staying safe in a risky world. As a parent, I'm responsible for both keeping my children safe and preparing them to handle risks, challenges, and contradictions well. As a Christian, I need to guard my eyes, ears, emotions, imagination, and intellect from temptations to sin in order to watch out for the safety of my soul.

Some of the dangers are external, some internal. It would be as presumptuous to expose myself to pornography as to send my new driver into freeway traffic. But, somehow, in a world filled with porn (among the world's many dangers, this one seems most "in my face"), I must learn a dynamic balance—a freedom to move forward within tension, in the face of danger—without wrecking my soul. The approach to danger must take into account the maturity, or preparedness, of the person being trained. Only a person more advanced in the subject at hand can make this assessment well.

The role of wise elders, virtuous spiritual advisors, and great teachers in the becoming of a human person cannot be overestimated. You cannot see your own self in the light of experience or expertise you do not have. Your first learning will always be derived from, received from, those who are your superiors. Even if you are "self-taught," you learn by reading great books or by comparing your skills to standards set by more highly trained practitioners. A mentor or leader is, like a placenta, part of the environmental structure that supports your growth in freedom. They've got to push you past your comfort zone—into risky territory—to help you grow.

You, and your children, and all who are "at the beginning" of a learning curve of some sort, are vulnerable. You need to be open to

19 – Safety vs. Risk

direction from someone, yet protected from error and misdirection. You need to learn to trust and open yourself, to have a humble, teachable spirit—a task that can be especially daunting for anyone whose trust has ever been violated. Your own self-protective mechanisms may have helped in the short run, but they will cripple you in the long run. Education and formation in freedom always involves the tension of the safety–risk paradox.

Protect Us from Error

You (or your students) must develop skills to face higher-level challenges (even dangers), yet *only* facing them will teach you those skills. You will fail, but you must take the risk when it is a reasonable risk for which you are prepared. The area of study perhaps most critical for your soul's formation (and thus, one fraught with high risk) is doctrine. You've got to learn it from people who have their own flaws in understanding or communicating it. In this area, more than in driver's education, for example, the person of the teacher is of great importance. We teachers cannot avoid communicating self with all our lessons. (I should say "good teachers," as the reason many teachers are not good ones is that they withhold self, or try to.)

The more deeply a subject reaches into the level of the soul's formation, from the more external to the intermediate level of intellectual skill-building, and then still more inwardly, the more deeply formative will be the pattern of the teacher's own soul. Persons "bear" other persons within themselves and are deeply affected by the "imprint" of whoever resides within their hearts. Remember that every *form* exerts some pressure upon those who receive it to conform to its own organizing principles, values, or message. Your education occurs constantly as the patterns you ingest "teach" you to conform.

In this light, the reality of Christ's own emergence as perfect pattern within my soul strikes me as the highest model for great teachers. With catechism classes as with driving lessons, the movement from unequivocally "safe" to possibly dangerous encounters must correspond to the maturation of judgment and skill. The driver moves gradually into the turbulence of traffic, and the new (or young, or untutored) believer into the turbulence of ideas. The scope of the sphere within which you operate freely grows as you grow. I call that sphere "freedom," "self," "being." Excellent catechesis becomes an internal support structure for opening and expanding that territory.

Life-to-Life Transfer

The movement toward maturity necessarily involves exposure to comparison, competition, scrutiny, criticism. You cannot grow in your capacity to negotiate the turbulence or bear the tension of this world's challenges unless you try and fail many, many times under careful guidance. When faced with failure, the strength of your emotional fabric is also tested. You may be able to laugh off ineptitude at math or chess, but when you fail miserably on a test in your major field or humiliate yourself during some public performance, your self-concept is at stake. The temptation is to flinch from trying again when emotional discomfort, or tension, turns the learning curve into a treacherous mountain.

Even worse, when you look into an argument against the Faith and fail to know how to address it, your discomfort may extend into a spiritual crisis. Many students form emotional bonds with people who despise the Faith, and then they have grave difficulties bearing the tension between love's open receptivity and wisdom's wariness. To reject an argument may feel like a rejection of a beloved friend, relative, or teacher. We've got to teach and learn a) the subject at hand, b) how to take criticism and failure, and c) how to approach argument in a way that does not violate the person who challenges our thinking. These tasks correspond to the first, second, and third dimensions of a person's formation: The Way of the Child, The Way of Youth, and The Way of Maturity.

Learning to take in content is called the "grammar stage" in classical education. First, the mind is ordered to words and their meaning. Simple information transfer is a foundation for higher education. In the "dialectic stage," a person develops the emotional resilience and capacity for tension necessary to practice the new skill and fail, argue key points with others, dig deeper, deal with paradox, and engage the

19 – Safety vs. Risk

self more fully with the subject matter. Maturity corresponds to the "rhetoric stage." You develop the capacity to communicate what you have appropriated, what you have made your own, in a way that involves your own, personal response to the material.

At its highest, rhetoric leads to poetry, moves from argument to art. The greater the fullness and freedom of your self, the more communication approaches communion—self-donation, the life-to-life transfer, the art of teaching exemplified by Christ. The capacity of the student, or audience, to receive affects the fullness of this transfer. The de-formation of the soul compromises, or retards, this capacity. You can teach "true things," but unless these truths are given place within the listener to sprout and grow, they fall on stony, weedy ground, accomplishing very little.

20 – Intention vs. Attention

Place Your Interest Here

IF YOU ARE NOT INTERESTED, no amount of lecturing about a subject will actually transfer the teacher's knowledge or wisdom into your brain. The lengths to which teachers are willing to go to "get you interested" show how important your participation is to the success of an educational exchange. They'll try to "make it relevant," hoping to engage your self-interest; "make it attractive," using your desire to possess what seems good and beautiful; "make it hands-on," knowing your mind is likely to become interested in what your body experiences; and "make it snappy," hoping you'll take the medicine as long as you can get it over with quickly.

All these well-meant efforts to coax you to invest yourself may work, but they may also reinforce a dangerous message. If you learn, along with whatever subject is being taught, that you should interest yourself most in what concerns you most, or in what is most pleasurable, or in that which you can touch, or if you get the idea that the subject matter is like an awful medicine, you'll receive some de-formation along with the new material. Messages like these work at the deeper level of the soul's formation while your body and intellect are taking in the information at the surface. It may take years of accumulated repetition for these, and other, messages to shape your attitude toward learning.

What if, instead, students were told this: "Your interest is something you decide, in freedom, to place into the essence of whatever you want to learn fully. See if you can, with a free act of will, interest yourself in what I am teaching. This is a potentially powerful faculty, and you must exercise it to strengthen it. I don't interest you—you do. This will be very hard and take lots of time to learn to do well." Many people never achieve the capacity to place their own minds right into the midst of ideas as though extending self right into form to grasp it.

20 – Intention vs. Attention

Can I Have Your Attention?

They learn, instead, a collection of facts, a plot summary, a scientific description, the moral of the story—all of which flatten the lived encounter with reality into the experience of taking in a symbol of reality to file away. If you return from a trip and realize you've been behind a camera most of the time, you'll see why the two-dimensional experience is second best. If you have pages of notes with many of the teacher's exact words but have to reread them all for a clue to what was said, you've been clutching at the image of knowledge while you might have simply entered into it and let it be re-presented within your own mind as a present reality.

Unfortunately, most attempts to lure your interest, your in-*tension*, by which you reach out actively to grasp and affect reality, are actually bids for your *attention*. The world is chock-full of lighted signs, flashing cartoon characters, gorgeous movie stars—most trying to get a few precious seconds in which to imprint a product preference or an action imperative. Traffic signals, bumper stickers, tattoos, loud noises, catchy tunes, all play to the childlike passive receptivity of your attention. Your eyes are attracted to movement, for instance, so television camera operators increase the number of visual events per minute more and more—ratcheting up the frenzy to attract your eye and get you to stay tuned for the commercial message.

It's delightful, in a way, to be entertained by the sights and sounds around you. Attention opens you to reality, stops you in wonder. You focus upon the object of attention—affected by it, taking it in. But your attention is being seduced as you move between the Scylla of sensory shutdown and the Charybdis of sensory overload. Whether you implode, explode, go numb, or get lost in a frenzy of attending to more than your mind can process, you lose.

Superficial attention-grabbers actually bypass your power of willingly interesting yourself in reality, and they weaken it as a result. They operate much as a bribe for good behavior operates to weaken a child's self-control. Think of how closely tied most of these are to a call-to-quick-action: Buy now! Push this button… Call 1-800… Click… Like… Friend. Somebody values your power to act—buy, vote, give—but not your power to act freely.

Souls at Work

Let's Get Engaged

Where your mind might get engaged (moving you toward freedom), the enemy's tactic is confusion. You try to figure out—the best diet, the right candidate, the real repercussions, the truth about the issues—but are so overwhelmed by conflicting explanations that the mind gives up. Is this "mental despair" a sin? I think not, but it results in a similar impotence. Clarity remains just beyond reach not because truth cannot be known but because your interest in this area does not extend into its depths, its essences, through the gauntlet of obfuscations.

Let's review: Your kids won't learn actively unless they learn the power of intention; they won't learn passively (sad, because wonder is the root of education) unless they learn the power of attention. You will not be free as long as you stay confused about reality, or truth. You are "not free" to the extent others manipulate your attention. When you react to any demand for action without first consulting self and a fuller picture of reality (one that includes your bank balance, competing claims on your time, alternative ways of responding, other sources of information, or the teachings of the Church, for example), you are acting in less-than-full freedom. Stop clicking the "bondage buttons" and start creating your own freedom! Lucky for you, the plethora of invitations to slavery around you can become an abundance of opportunities to practice freedom. Truly, God works all things together for your good.

21 – Delight vs. Discipline

You've Got to Want It

How MANY TIMES will kids trudge up a hill for the thrill of sledding down? What delights us has such attractive power that we willingly "do the work," whatever it is and however arduous it may be. It can be a little scary, though, to give your child, or yourself, free rein to move at will, follow passions, invest effort to make dreams come true. Because you know there's also danger in such freedom, you hesitate, withhold full approval, stop short of the glorious freedom of flying down your particular hill. The checking caused by self-conscious inhibition can lead to the very disaster you fear. A self-fulfilling prophecy of disaster deepens your fear of following where desire leads.

There's also the danger of wrongful desire. You can't ignore the reality of your own flawed motivation, the ambiguity of your best aspirations, and the nasty way your sinful self intrudes into and twists selfless deeds to selfish purposes. "Wait till I'm pure of heart," you seem to say, "and then I'll be safe to follow my desires." "I want only to be holy," you might add, as though that absolves you of responsibility for your own talents, desires, and dreams.

Perhaps you wait, inwardly, for a sign of God's approval, or a sense of certainty that the outcome of your actions will be positive. Then the complex mind may turn again, realizing how easily such images as "a sign from God" or "great results" are generated to support self-will. "Be simple!" says your spiritual director. But where is the path of simplicity in the forest of self-doubt, conflicting scenarios, and mutually exclusive claims upon your time and energy? How can you take in all this "reality" (even throwing out the "vain imaginings" of the future) and come up with an action plan that enlarges your freedom, your sphere of response-ability?

But What Does God Want?

How much easier it would be simply to obey. If only someone in legitimate authority over you would tell you what to do next, you could relax all the interior tension and do even the hardest task in simplicity. Most of us, however, have no such person in charge. We must give authority—to a personal trainer, a professor, a doctor, a spiritual director, a financial planner, a diet book—to get help accomplishing our own goals. And then, we rebel! It's hard to accept discipline, even when you freely assent to the "boss" of some aspect of your life. The simple path of obedience is complicated—again—by the interior struggle to figure out whose will is really being done, and how to do it without losing the power of free agency. Prayer will surely help in all this decision making, but not necessarily because God sends an unmistakable sign pointing the way.

Parents and teachers want both to harness the energy of delight and to provide the invaluable support of discipline for the sake of their students. The challenge of balancing those aims gives you insight into God's own parenting. His yoke may be easy and His discipline a form of love, but you'll have to learn to stand in the face of buffeting storms and endure suffering that seems like child abuse to onlookers. He wants to give you the desires of your heart, let you run freely in the path of His commands, and give you life abundant, but He serves up a program of mortification of desire, falling on the path, and voluntary poverty. Talk about a paradox!

How to Win the Tug-of-War

The mental whirlwind that results as such thoughts take up their tug-of-war within you has a still point—let's see if we can find it. At the center of a parent's dilemma are the well-being, development, and eventual freedom of his child. At the center of God's focus, are yours. The steady reference that can help calm the storm and resolve the tension between delight and discipline is freedom. The more external discipline you can *freely* accept, the more support for your own freedom you will internalize. The key is to learn to engage self in free action, even when the marching orders are given by rightful, or merely powerful, authority.

21 – Delight vs. Discipline

Saint Maximilian Kolbe's free act of self-sacrifice not only saved the one man he replaced in the death chamber but also invited every single witness—Nazi guard and prisoners alike—to a freedom that inheres in the human person and is not dependent upon any freedoms controlled by external structures. It is dangerous to be obedient *as* a slave—to thoughtlessly follow every order (whether of advertisers or appetites, priests or peers) without the engagement of your own freedom.

Are the obligations imposed by the Church, the decisions of parents, the laws of society, then, oppressive of personal freedom? No more so than the rules of music notation, grammar, aerodynamics, or courtesy. These external structures of "control" have no power to rob you of interior freedom. You are able, by learning to say "yes" only in true freedom, to enlarge your freedom—not in spite of but rather with the aid of external strictures, disciplines, and limitations!

It is also dangerous to move forward—to drive, to eat, to offer service, to create a work of art—without considering your self's true goals, preferences, desires, and ideas. The realization of *you* depends on your free responses to both interior and exterior reality. The clear internal "form" of what you want to accomplish by your efforts needs time to develop. When you speed past the step of attending to the development of this form, your will engages to generate only vaguely understood goals, often working against your true desires. Nonaction is a critical skill.

As teachers, we can help students take (and practice) response-ability by allowing time for and recalling their attention to this interior "place" or "pause" where discipline meets desire, tension must be resolved, and action (the free engagement of the will) responds to reality. The same action can work at a deep or a superficial level, depending upon the depth of interior engagement, or freedom. The process of developing this awareness—of interior tension, of desire, of what it feels like to act in true freedom—*is* the process of truly growing up.

Whatever discipline you willingly embrace—learn to play the piano, go on a pilgrimage, abstain from chocolate, try to win that track meet—serves to strengthen your soul's capacity for freedom, to the extent you appropriate the discipline for that purpose. Just as passive suffering can be "wasted" if you forget your power to offer it as prayer, action can be "wasted" if you forget your power to engage and respond instead of reacting. Remember the proposal: exercise your power to wield yourself according to your own desires and yield yourself according to God's. Then, teach others to do the same—invite them to the glorious freedom of the children of God!

FORMS
Structures Worth Exploring

Proposed: That forms, as embodiments of the responses and judgments of their makers, invite you to enter into, to explore, not only the form but also the minds, values, longings, and experiences of those makers. Your capacity to see through form to the being, the need or yearning from which it emerged, is enlarged with each attempt. Form is, then, an invitation to you to exercise and enlarge your freedom: the sphere of your response-ability.

In each of the following chapters, I explore an example of "form"— a resolution of some combination of tensions that invites entrance, participation, sharing of original experience, or acceptance of a gift. We usually only scratch the surface of the forms around us and haven't the time or capacity to take in the "all" that any form represents. In Tensions, your intellect, primarily, was engaged. In Frames, your capacity for wonder, or for affective response, was invited. In this section, I hope to place you into a more "three-dimensional" encounter with the creative responses of others and so to stimulate you to act in accordance with your own best interests, and the interests of those you serve. If you are not accustomed to looking with wonder—suspending judgment for the space of encounter—you will be less able to draw wealth from forms. If you have not practiced dealing with tensions, you will be tempted to accept forms unconsciously, or reject them mindlessly. Forms are graduate schools of tension. If your desire is to invite others to freedom, keep reading!

Notes on Growing Up – Wealth:
The Way of Maturity and the Third Dimension of Freedom

Wealth: the capacity to appropriate treasure from the structures where it is stored and to rejoice in its constructive distribution. Talents, wisdom, material possessions, ideas, love, spiritual gifts, and knowledge are among the treasures of the wealthy. The wealth of a child is relatively "uninvested," an unrealized potentiality. Because children lack distinct boundaries or definition, their "wealth" escapes like water from a leaky pitcher and spills willy-nilly over those lucky enough to be near them. My point is that full *realization of wealth, or abundance, is a quality of maturity. It implies the development of a capacity not only to receive deeply but also to contain, possess, maintain, and steward resources in order to give them freely. Maturation and fruition go together, as do youth and growth, or infancy and dependence.*

Problematic models of "growing up" contribute to difficulties with this third dimension. If you are a "powerless point," a one-dimensional being with little power to exercise your will in action or to restrain the action of your will, you may have an effect in the world, but it will likely be self-serving, or destructive. If you are a two-dimensional "pointless power," the distribution of your wealth will follow the narrow, taut lines of tension and self-interest—wealth distributed, if at all, with stress, struggle, and limited effectiveness.

The hyper-child, as we've seen, has little power to retain, cultivate, or distribute wealth. The hyper-adult, thinking of his wealth as the goal and end product of his own efforts and investments, or the proof of his value, is likely to have neglected the development of a capacity to give that wealth freely. He may be restricted to channels of commercial distribution, for instance. Whether he is "plucked" like a flower, or bought and used like a product, he misses out on the joy of free self-donation.

Wealth is also stored up around us in the structures others have made. It is a sad reality that often only the "wealthy" have the capacity to appropriate more wealth. A child may experience a concert with delight, but an adult should receive even more. Delight, beauty, attraction—all provide the initial impetus to draw near, or to approach something. As an adult, you also bring well-formed intellect (memory, expertise, analysis) to bear upon the object you consider.

To receive the most from the forms given by others (their self-statements, gestures, works of art, institutions), you must look through what is received as form to what is given as being*—understanding that there is a veil, an impediment to seeing perfectly. This is an "objectivity" that allows the "object" to be itself, not one that reduces it so as to render it small or unthreatening. You consider both the form and what you can receive of the person, ideas, meaning behind it. Like the object beam that helps form a hologram, your mind seeks simply to know the form as it is. The greater your development toward the highest values for this form, the greater will be the extent to which you experience tension between it and the ideal-of-it. For example: the music teacher hears the student's recital more fully than the parent, given her greater objective development in musical form.*

The more the emotions are affected, the greater is the interior tension that must be borne to move through the form to the argument, meaning, or intention behind it. In this sense, the parent is hearing the same recital more deeply than the teacher. This is a "subjectivity" that allows the affection of the subject/viewer to color what is known about the object, or form, being considered. Like the gaze of Christ, the heart's perspective interferes with what is known objectively. Like the reference beam forming a hologram, this doubled sight creates an interference pattern that must be interpreted to be resolved.

Within this form are held someone's answers to a question, or questions. If you don't get much out of it, it may be because you haven't asked the questions—haven't felt a need-to-know that corresponds to the argument, or solution, embodied there. You may also miss much of what is available from the form if you do not resolve the tension, interpret the interference pattern, render a judgment, make a response.

A child may drink deeply of form because he is deeply affected by it. With no interference from education, he simply is present to it and receives it whole. The youth, or one growing intellectually in the apprehension of such forms, may draw from it a great deal because experience, education, practice have enlarged his capacity. The "adult" (not by age, but by the fullness of well-integrated affect and intellect—emotional and mental faculties) should have the greatest capacity to receive from form whatever wealth it contains. The child may not be conscious of encountering God in this form. The one who is struggling through the tensions this form presents may forget to cry out to God for help. The adult may have a rich experience, but unless the Spirit is invited to help create a response, the experience will not be as fully dimensional as possible.

Having opened to this reality and made an informed (generated deep within, heart-affected) judgment, you then render it, represent it, communicate it. Responding in some way to the encounter with form, you deepen your experience of it, retain and make use of it, and make it accessible to others—spreading the wealth. This is the way of maturity, developed through practice with forms.

You should feel no pressure whatsoever to enter into any forms. Read everything here about the riches available in forms, and be even more amazed that you have everything possible in the Eucharist! Unless forms are approached as means to realize more fully what He is, what He has already given, you'll miss the point. No one can appropriate it all, understand everything, move freely in every area. Education isn't, or shouldn't be, about amassing more knowledge or experience; rather, it is about being able to know, love, and serve Him through the limited means of self. Those means can be cultivated, expanded, made more receptive and responsive, but that all pales before Christ's own power to raise Himself up within you! Go, have fun in forms, but don't let them become a burden.

22 – Maps, Models, Methods

A "FORM" may be so familiar you've never stopped to think of it as a created expression of another person's judgments, or as an invitation to enter and experience reality. A map, for instance, folded and tattered in your car's door pocket, may sit unused for months at a time. When, finally, you need help locating yourself in space, you take for granted the amazing correspondence of this graphical world to the physical territory you need to navigate. You want to get from point A to point B, or to restore your sense of clarity about your location. You aren't particularly interested in the history of cartography, the skill of surveying, or the mind of the geographer.

Like most people with most forms, you have an intersection with the surface expression—the map—and the encounter needn't deepen much at all. Your reality is touched in a fleeting way, but you are not drawn in to the experience of, or the being of, those who made the form. They may actually be so remote from the form—especially if it is a mechanical reproduction—as to seem inaccessible.

Such is life. It may be enough just to realize there are such depths awaiting your exploration—in forms all around you. Like the two-dimensional road map, a three-dimensional model may guide your perception of some "territory" you are navigating. Architects construct building models to work with spatial relationships, materials selection, and site planning. Computer design programs generate complex construction diagrams and allow seemingly infinite manipulation—extending (or dwarfing, by comparison) the mind's capacity to hold elements in tension. Mathematicians, market researchers, economists, and physicists model reality with computer power to discern relationships and connections imperceptible to the unaided mind.

Various healing modalities collect the wisdom of ages—the experienced-then-communicated reality of many persons—into forms. Ayurveda, homeopathy, herbal lore, and Chinese traditional medicine are all models through which the reality of the dis-eased human body is helped toward health. Each approach suggests different responses to the same symptoms, because each embodies different experiences, questions, presuppositions, and values. All are also quite different from the allopathic or "medical" model that most of us find familiar.

All too often in the history of healing, the unfamiliar model has been discounted as too foreign, too ancient, too strange, too hard to understand. Each form has its own grammar—new definitions to learn, odd new ways of using old words, even variations in the basic framework of the body's systems—and its own logic that must be learned just to enter, experience, and evaluate it. Those who do enter must turn and communicate, or re-present, the forms to outsiders. Gradually, as such representations make these huge bastions of wisdom more accessible, medical-model physicians are integrating some old insights into new treatment protocols. Practitioners of alternate healing modalities are welcome also to the wealth of information made possible through the more analytical, science-based model. The forms remain distinct, even as they influence one another through individuals willing to move deeply into understanding.

Models for thinking about money affect philanthropy. A grant-seeker must find and articulate a good "fit" between his plans to use money and a donor's ideas about how money fuels action in the world. Microlenders think small, personal, temporary giving is most empowering and effective. Some foundations only give large grants to well-established agencies. Others look at financial giving in a more entrepreneurial way and see applicants through a more venture capital-style lens. People looking for help must first realize that these mental maps exist, or they will bark up a lot of wrong trees as they seek financial support for their good works.

Personality style and learning style models help us to articulate reality that is otherwise difficult to comprehend and then to navigate, think, and plan better in that ordered awareness. We know the map cannot fully convey the wholeness, the real-ness of a person, but these lenses are valuable forms to look through to see self, or another, more clearly. The better our map, or model, corresponds

22 – Maps, Models, Methods

to reality and the more fully that reality is conveyed, the more helpful it will be as in-formation that prompts a fitting response.

Each form is a lens to see through—introducing its own distortions, but also illuminating reality in a unique way. Models, as ordered frameworks for approaching some aspect of reality, are powerful aids to thinking minds. As invisible lenses shaped by philosophical, theological, and moral presuppositions, they can cause blind spots for the unreflective viewer. You don't see anything without some mediating structure. There is no perfect objectivity, because your own emotions and memory act as filters through which you perceive reality. The goal of thinking "formally" about the lenses you see through is not to become so hyperaware of them that you can't see through them at all but simply to realize that your experience of, and formation by, reality is affected, or colored, to some extent.

Because much of your formal education occurred when you were a child, you may not have ever looked beyond the system of instruction to the model from which it emerged. Much less likely are you to have looked backward through that model so as to understand its presuppositions, its historical development, or the people behind it, with all their own experiences and values. As an adult, you may want to ask more questions, because—in a way—you are still looking at education (your own, your children's and students') through that lens. Your negative or positive emotional connections with that particular form add "color" or "spin" to the way you now approach education. You are formed not only by the content of your education but also by the context—the model, environment, or form that carries a message also has the power to in-form you. Again, you'd go crazy trying to overanalyze your own formation, but it can be freeing to have some awareness of these early, less conscious influences.

Jean Piaget, Maria Montessori, Jean-Jacques Rousseau, John Dewey, Don Bosco, Shin'ichi Suzuki, and hundreds of other educators have come up with vastly different educational models. Ancient scholars, medieval monks, and modern unschoolers have formed their insights into others. Frederick Alexander, Moshe Feldenkrais, Joseph Pilates, and others have created models for "body education"

Souls at Work

and self-awareness. You can't dig into them all, but in forming your own response, some attention to the formulations of others is helpful.

Educational models give answers directly or indirectly to the questions posed in Tensions. Your own answers to those questions will help you enter into and understand whichever other educational models you study. Each form you explore gives you a concrete way of exercising your capacity for tension as it raises new questions or gives new answers to the questions you've been asking.

All the models we've discussed derive their strength from the degree to which they correspond to reality and their effectiveness from the degree to which they produce the results you want when you act in accordance with them. There will be things you agree with and things you don't, pieces that resonate with other things you've learned and those that conflict with any model you explore. The accuracy of a map or model grows as it is tested in the sphere of action. You must "test" the models against the reality of your own lived experience, in the sphere of your own actions.

The more fully formed the model, the harder it is for its proponents to acknowledge discrepancies, errors, or problems and then make revisions or adjust for new conditions. The more the model you see through corresponds to reality-as-you-know-it, the more it becomes, like your family of origin, hard to separate from your own identity. Because of this tendency to shut out anything that does not correspond to the model, it becomes a self-fulfilling prophecy of what you will experience as reality.

Just as the "classics" of literature have qualities that transcend particular time periods, the "classical" model, though it originated in ancient Greece, influenced much that followed, and it continues to in-form new developments in education. Its trivium (grammar, dialectic, rhetoric) is a sort of fractal for human growth and the growth of human institutions. Indeed, this book could be titled *Human Growth to Freedom, Explored through the Lens of the Classical Trivium*—if that weren't so unwieldy.

The grammar stage of the classical model corresponds to the first stage of growth in any subject you tackle, or in the life of a child, or in the formation of a human institution. First, you must learn the

22 – Maps, Models, Methods

language of any new area of study. A child claims the world by naming it and learning to use words in the basic grammatical constructions that give him access to information about reality. A nonprofit board writes its mission statement, defines the way certain terms will be understood for its bylaws, and establishes the structure through which to act upon the world. You grow in freedom as you exercise your capacity to place your interest into the essence, the grammar, of new realities.

The dialectic stage corresponds to the second dimension of growth. You must engage with, grapple with, argue with the "givens" in order to move deeper into the experience of the reality you encounter. You could spend all day immersed in a new language and grow in the understanding of many basic words and constructions. Until you struggle to use it, though, you have not "grown up" into this second dimension.

You learn your faith first by trust—reasonably receiving it as a given from parents and teachers. To make it your own, you must enter into its doctrines and arguments more fully. The interior logic of reality becomes apparent as you struggle to embrace seeming contradictions, compare what you see to what you have seen before, contrast what is in front of you with what you expected, and adjust the neat picture in your mind to account for the messy reality you encounter.

The rhetoric stage corresponds to the third dimension of growth —the power to re-present, to respond to, to communicate, to move freely in the reality you have internalized. In other words, the capacity for creating forms and for fully entering into created forms is the work of this third stage. The dancer works for many hours to fly "effortlessly" across the floor. The artist's preliminary sketches become a finished painting. The saint finally gives himself with complete abandon to the poor he once struggled to love.

As a whole, the trivium corresponds to the phase I am calling the "way of youth" in this book. This work of learning to use words to articulate and reflect upon, and then to convey, reality is where most of us will spend most of our lives in most spheres of reality. In general, life itself is a long field of such struggle between a "childhood" of simple receptivity to and an eternity of profound experience of the Real. In the classical model of education, the formal trivium was preceded by a childhood of poetic and gymnastic development. Its sequel was the education made possible by the struggle to learn how to learn. In the quadrivium (what we consider "college level"), the forms present in the created world and re-presented by man were made accessible through study of mathematics, geometry, astronomy, and music.

Stratford Caldecott has described the classical model beautifully in *Beauty for Truth's Sake* and *Beauty in the Word* and has shown its compatibility with other educational models. It is worthwhile to look at any other model with the classical model in mind, to see what correspondences and divergences there are between the two. See the Appendices for a further conversation with him about choosing the best form of education and creating new forms. There is no such thing as a "pure" education in any one model, since there is inevitable cross-pollination between them and since each expression of a model of thought will be "colored" by many other cultural factors that form its context—the reality to which it corresponds.

Model leads to method—an additional layer of form that may or may not correspond perfectly (in realization) to the ideals formulated in the model. Therefore, if you plan to delve into, for instance, the Montessori model, please don't go visit a local "Montessori" school and assume that their expression of the model is an accurate representation. The writings of the model's founder or of initial theorists can be examined, but derivative works may be more accessible. For example, Charlotte Mason's writings on education run to six volumes, but Karen Andreola's *A Charlotte Mason Companion* does a great job of condensing and clarifying it all for today's reader.

As you explore, take time to notice the tensions, resonances, likes and dislikes, arguments and agreements, reactions and frustrations that occur within you as you are affected by the forms you enter. Try to work in some concrete experience of the models that interest you. Sit in on a class, visit a school, or talk to students and teachers training to use this model. Some you may only be able to experience through books, such as the monastic model or the autodidact's eclectic life story.

Along the way, as you "digest" or "process" the influences of others, your own growth toward freedom will occur. You can't possibly take in everything before making your own judgments, creating your own forms. Not everyone is aiming for an academic comprehensiveness as they dig into a field of interest. Amateur dabbling is a valid approach—more conducive to incorporation of your personal response—and often opens the door to deeper involvement.

One small aspect may attract your interest, as a rabbit hole may lead into a wonderland, or you may aim for a broader overview. The lens of attention adjusts for "near" and "far," "wide" and "narrow" focus, like the lens of your eye. Simply the realization that forms are three-dimensional invites you to freely choose your depth of focus and enjoy each exploration more fully.

23 – Journey

You don't usually think of a journey as a created form. If you're the kid being towed along in your parents' travels, then, for you, journey is a more "one-dimensional" experience. Creating a journey can, itself, be a structured expression of your values and yearnings, your answers to questions, your resolution of tension. Those who come along, and those who experience the journey vicariously through your slides, blog, or conversation, do enter a "form" of sorts and can explore beyond its boundaries to the mystery of its maker.

Though in this sense the journey itself can be a form, here we will look at the journey as a means, a way of entering into the form of other cultures and into the experience of life as a dialogue with strangers.

In this light, the whole world—especially that which you enter "as a stranger"—becomes a form generated by others, embodying their history, values, and desires. Every aspect—the stores, signs, language, gestures, traditions, foods—draws you toward these mysterious others. They may or may not welcome you. It is a curious reality that, since we are inescapably exposed to the alien in our midst, we may feel vulnerable, defensive, even hostile about his presence. Our cultural expressions, our outward-facing selves, will be characterized by our degree of transparency, of hospitality.

The form you are in as you travel is so densely layered as to be practically impenetrable. You may scratch the surface and feel a sense of "knowing" this place, these people, but unless you stay a while, embracing the tensions this journey presents, you know only as a child knows. You'll have deep impressions, emotional associations, great memories, and real admiration for the territory you pass through. Can you just stop and marvel at the beauty of the alps, a statue, a costume, or a cityscape? Let yourself just drink it in without trying to understand, label, categorize, or judge. You'll flatten out the journey if you remain unaffected in this basic, childlike way. You surely don't want to become just a walking guidebook,

23 – Journey

experiencing the world around you without the sort of delight that is made possible by your capacity to wonder.

If you struggle to learn the language, overcome cross-cultural prejudices and misunderstandings, or make it your business to learn more about the history and culture, your experience will be more fully fleshed-out. Do you wonder what that sign means? Dig out your dictionary, or—better—ask a local for help. Do move, though, into the second dimension. Find something worth chewing on and do the work of digging deeper, trying to understand more fully, pushing yourself to explore beyond mere curiosity through some fuller study. Ask questions and let the answers lead you to more questions.

What does it take to enter journey as a form—a three-dimensional, multisensory experience of place and persons? As with every form: wonder, struggle, and then response. When you have someone who shares your experience, response is almost effortless. So, on your journey, cultivate relationships. Share your reflections about whatever you encounter—in conversation, in letters home, in blog posts. Strengthen old friendships, and look around for new friends. The better able you are to invite others to know you and to interest yourself in them—their ideas, needs, frustrations, etc.—the more fully you will experience any new territory.

The form of a journey takes shape within your own being as you move through the "materials" it is made of. Like a living museum, you are filled with artifacts of experience. The associations you form with persons will give greater solidity to the representation you retain within. Germany will not be just a place on a map or a mental picture of castles, pubs, and red tile roofs; rather, it will become a three-dimensional lived experience linked to the personal interactions and emotional memories you store with the images.

The "new territory" you "travel" in can be a new workplace, a stay in the hospital, or a freshman year at college. Allow any of these to take the form of "journey," and your experience will be richer. You are going to feel like a stranger, learn some words in a new language, encounter the mixed attitudes of the natives, interest yourself in the strange culture, and struggle to meet your own needs in the new context.

But first, stop and be affected. Observe your heart's initial response—what attracts and what is repulsive here? Consider your feelings of fear and anxiety. Ask God for the grace to release self-protective defenses where they are not actually needed. What delights you? Notice now, before it all becomes familiar and prosaic. One of the gifts of exploring unfamiliar territory is the sharpening of the senses.

You may have a heightened awareness of signs, gestures, smells, facial expressions, and sounds as your mind works to construct a mental map without the familiar words and signals that usually are its building blocks. You'll find that your ability to sense meaning is a function of your whole being. The greater your capacity to integrate sensory and intellectual apprehension—feeling with information, heart with mind—the more fully response-able you will be. This is what it means to journey in freedom, toward freedom.

A pilgrimage is a particular sort of journey—one whose contribution to your formation has much to do with your depth of interest in the experience as a conversation with God. Any journey can be taken in the spirit of pilgrimage, as you consciously offer the trials and tribulations as prayer and seek amid the events and personal encounters to be acted upon by the Lord. If your journey can include visits to churches, shrines, and other pilgrimage sites, so much the better, but your intention is a factor in the transformation.

Consider education as "journey" for rich insights. Are you focused on one particular destination or traveling through a series of must-see sights? Do you prepare meticulously with guidebooks and research or jump into direct experience with no preconceived notions, maps, or guidance? Exploring this metaphor can help you see why you resolve all the tensions of travel/education the way you do, and how your responses affect your experience. Some teachers will be companions on the educational journey, others tour guides or translators. Parent-educators may take a different approach to each subject, each child, or each school year.

Life itself is most frequently linked to the journey metaphor, but for most of us life is too long, too familiar, to be lived fully as such. G.K. Chesterton's character Innocent Smith goes "around the world" just to experience—briefly, as a stranger—the wonder and

23 – Journey

freshness of returning home and seeing his wife anew. Each of us journeys through many different forms, looks through many lenses, to reach our eternal destiny. We create some of them—our dreams of what may be, our castles in the air. Those intermediate forms are necessary, valuable, and real—they attract us onward, forward, higher—but they mustn't substitute for that return to Home.

The more complex and dense with meaning a form is, the more likely we are to just look "at" it instead of see through it, move into it. In its richness, it can overwhelm and seem to shut out our participation. We are told in Scripture to "cast down vain imaginations" (2 Corinthians 10:5; also translated "reasonings," "arguments"), as they can actually interfere with our engagement with reality. The mind that can generate whole worlds of imaginary experience is in danger of being cut off from the difficulties of real experience and gradually becomes more susceptible to the easy fulfillment of vain imagination. The artist capable of producing the most heavenly music from an organ or cello is in danger of allowing the delights of created beauty to surfeit his desire for heavenly beauty.

How, instead, do we ensure that the experience of intermediate form continues to lead us (or our students) through to the greater good? If our journeys are to take us to our true destiny, they must always lead home. Ultimately all derivative forms must "bend the knee" to Christ, must be humbled as means to His ends for us. The most fully dimensional *real*-ization of any form is this shining through of heaven that occurs when we open experience to God's companionship. If you cower at the dangers of travel, of beauty, of form, you do not learn to move back and forth freely in the three-dimensional territory that is your own being.

Ideally, a person grows "three-dimensionally"—as a point of light shining outward in a sphere of personhood, moving toward his destiny, expanding, integrating, and shining brighter all along the way. Reality—forms—call him out of himself toward all that is. The beauty that wounds him, in a way, throws him off balance. The experience of wonder puts him in a new relationship with himself—a second seeing, a binocular vision that enables self-reflection and self-evaluation. As he grows, he learns to understand what attracts him, to know it more fully, to struggle to possess it. Finally, he gains the freedom to move through music, foreign countries, the Church, educational models, complex systems—through form—freely.

What you learn anywhere, at any stage, in any "dimension," informs you and calls you forward toward your final destiny through all realities. Your growing freedom is the insurance against getting stuck, or trapped, or seduced into substituting the greatness of created form for the superabundant greatness of the One in whom all form lives and moves and has being. This is a journey to enjoy thoroughly… bon voyage!

24 – Books

BOOKS ARE AMONG my favorite "forms" to enter into and to explore. A book is, clearly, a framework, or lens, through which we can enter not just a subject of interest but also an author's passion and personality. Through a carefully constructed, one-way conversation with someone who longs to convey information, story, argument, or experience, you have a lived encounter with that material from the "inside," in a way. You hear the voice of a real person and submit your own seeing to his eyes—not mindlessly, but as unreservedly as possible in order to see as he sees. If you cannot muster a teachable spirit (for nonfiction) or a willing suspension of disbelief (for fiction), then you will be holding yourself back, to some degree, from fully receiving the book.

It takes skill to read well—skill that doesn't "come naturally," without self-awareness or instruction. Mortimer Adler's *How to Read a Book* is the classic work for would-be readers. You can learn phonics and produce words—even understand them—from linked letters of the alphabet. You can also learn—per Adler—to read more effectively, taking into account the style of book, your own intentions, and the nature of the content. When you read most three-dimensionally, you will experience the text—and even the person of its author—as most fully re-presented within your own being.

This may sound like mumbo jumbo to you if you've not experienced it. Let me give an analogy. Have you ever looked into a "magic eye" poster (a muddled, distorted hodgepodge of color) and finally managed to perceive the shaped image that seems to emerge as you gaze "through" the poster? Once your mind "sees" the holographic, seemingly three-dimensional object, you can relax your stare and look all around the shape in near focus without losing it. It is present now, to your mind, as a whole entity, and you are free to explore its contours. These images remind me of Elisha: he prayed that his servant would realize that they were not at the mercy of an overwhelming enemy (2 Kings 6:17). The veil was lifted, his eyes were opened, and he perceived armies of angels encamped all around!

Reading like this strengthens the power of imagination. Though stories may seem more fully realized as movies, a movie is actually a reduction, a step down from the imagination's power to realize. When someone else takes over the imaginative function, our own interior dimension can atrophy and shrink. The development of the intellect facilitates your spiritual growth as it strengthens the "walls" of inner architecture that support open, free, spacious receptivity to reality.

A rich, three-dimensional experience of reading depends on your capacity and also on the quality of the book itself. Poorly written books *are* poor, partly because they do not correspond to the mind's disposition to build an interior "structure" with the building blocks of words it is given. Arguments that are not carefully developed or that have logical flaws undermine this interiorization of meaning. Actions inconsistent with character, implausible plot twists, and unnatural dialogue similarly frustrate the mind's attempts to hold on to a story-form and enter into it as a lived experience.

Some books will leave you cold if you have no patience for descriptions of scene and setting, no experience with complex interpersonal relationships, or an aversion to archaic forms of speech. Others you'll reject out of hand because you've already rejected the author's conclusion, premises, or person. One person's "passionate author" may be another's "ranting writer." Often, the only words that can resonate with you are those that confirm something you've already decided to agree with. So, you should be somewhat circumspect—are you agreeing because the author has mirrored your own conclusions, or are you disagreeing because you hate the author's hairdo?

Books that become three-dimensional forms for you are those that lead you *through* tension. You might avoid struggle and go right to the end for the author's final conclusion, the detective-reveals-who-done-it scene, or you might even settle for the plot summary on the back cover. With many books, then, you'll have a merely nodding acquaintance. To be more fully realized through reading,

24 – Books

though, you need to enter a few books more whole-ly. Even better, you'll reread some books many times.

A single book can be a place where you take a class from or have a conversation with an author. If his writing is lucid and his thoughts interest you, you leave the encounter with a new structure formed in your own mind. That structure can be excess furniture, cluttering up the place. It may even be a toe-stubbing stumbling block, interfering with your own thoughts. Or, you can use it as the basis for completely reorganizing your whole "interior space"—throwing out anything that clashes with it. You might—and this is better than thoroughly violating the existing order—dismantle it: use a few pieces now, save a few for pondering later, toss something that just won't work for you. A great book, "digested" by a person who has a great capacity for making good use of it, is a great teacher.

A. G. Sertillanges's *The Intellectual Life* is a book about cultivating this capacity to appropriate the riches present all around you in the form of books. Many have found in G. K. Chesterton the kind of faith-building intellectual conversation they longed for, in vain, within modern universities. Father James Schall, writing in recent times, has contributed to the self-education of many a reader by giving suggestions for further study of topics as diverse as politics and comedy. Lives have been deeply changed by the reading of J. R. R. Tolkien's epic *Lord of the Rings*. The *Catechism of the Catholic Church* is an amazing, multilayered, living book that invites a lifetime of exploration. Docility—a teachable spirit—is cultivated by reading your superiors. To be influenced—at least, to acknowledge that influence—takes humility.

To explore a book's footnotes (did you really think those were boring?) is an adventure. Each author leads you into his own reading—the process of his own formation—by way of quotations and citations. Literary allusions give you a similar glimpse into the reading experience of a fiction writer. You may realize that some degree of pre-reading is necessary to fully understand a book that builds upon a foundation of prior work. As with every sort of form, a book shuts you out and invites you in simultaneously. This is a critically important thing to understand, because otherwise you will simply feel that your way "in" is barred.

Some forms at least entertain you (a concert, a play), or feed you (a feast, the liturgy), or please you (a painting, a beautiful person), whether or not you have the capacity to receive them more fully. All forms, to some degree, both provide for and impede entrance. Some books will seem impossibly intimidating, and you'll find others more accessible. To grow, you need to take on some reading that challenges you to use and develop your intellectual capacity—hence the many lists of suggested reading for various age and ability levels made by educators with experience providing such challenges.

Three things bring a book to life: passion, presence, and voice. The author's passion for his subject should be conveyed—especially in books for children. If you read to a child, your own interest adds to this feeling that a subject is moving, affecting, powerful. Children can be taught that they will enjoy reading more when they bring their own interest into the experience of a book. Charlotte Mason is an educator/writer who has influenced many parents to seek out "living books" to share with their children.

Your presence as reader, the presence of an audience when reading is aloud, and the presence of the author help reading become a more three-dimensional experience. The author and illustrator have names. Noting them is a courtesy, a nod to authority, a sign of respect that the work of real persons mediated this encounter with reality, or this story, to you. Even the book designers made choices about type style, layout, and book size that you can notice, evaluate, and be thankful for. Gratitude is an interior response that makes any encounter more whole. Physical and mental presence can be increased by attention to the sensory elements of a text and by hearing the words within yourself as you read silently. There is evidence that the habit of hearing internally during reading can be cultivated and makes for a much-improved retention and understanding of what is read.

The "voice" of the reader-aloud is an obvious enrichment of the reading experience. Less obvious is the voice of the author, but it is no less important to a living book. The person reading aloud has a huge responsibility for reading well. Breath support, enunciation, posture, voices for characters, attention to punctuation—all are learnable ways to honor good writing. Writers strive to perfect their capacity to communicate meaning, so if you mediate their work to others, you have your work cut out for you. All the riches of story come to us through a history of orality that is important to preserve, especially in the experience of reading fiction. Poetry is meant to be heard. To read it well takes skill and practice. That work moves you from one- to two- to three-dimensional experience in the form, and the riches collected there.

Textbooks attempt to predigest a great deal of information and present it in a form that you may apprehend more readily. Too often, the committee approach to textbook writing results in a strangely unappealing amalgam of voices and perspectives. If you have found a subject hopelessly uninteresting, it may be because you simply have not found the subject discussed in the voice of an author who is genuinely passionate about it. Be careful to not let the form prejudice you against the reality it re-presents. Remember that your freedom is expanded as you learn to turn your attention to all reality and place your interest there—*int*o the *esse*nce of all that is.

Would it be preferable to learn only by direct experience and not indirectly through books? Though it is possible to go to extremes with reading, thus shutting out direct experience of reality, the opposite extreme of rejecting books altogether does not set you free. Books are among the "many counselors" who lead you to wisdom (Proverbs 11:14); they are doorways into places and times you cannot enter experientially and teachers who prepare you to make the most of the realities you can experience directly.

25 – Classes, Workshops, Seminars

EVERY FORM gets between you and some reality—mediates that reality to you and puts some spin, limits, distortion on what you see. The form can be invisible—a thought system, philosophical model, or prejudice grown "formal" through long habit. You may see only form and not sense any connection to reality beyond its boundaries—use the computer program without questioning the algorithms; glance at a framed photo and never wonder about the photographer. You may choose to enter form—attend a concert, participate in an improvisational comedy workshop—or be thrust in unwillingly or unconsciously, like Alice in her wonderland.

People taking classes are often present without much desire to be there, to learn the subject, or to engage with the teacher. Your experience of class-as-form may be negative, but once you're out of the compulsory education years, you'll likely return—again and again, and voluntarily—to that type of "orderly framework for encounter with reality." A good teacher is a very good thing. Formal instruction can be a delightful way to encounter new skills, information, or natural wonders. As a mediating structure, a good class, workshop, lecture, or seminar connects you with a carefully chosen subset of some reality in a way that, if it is effective, will create a re-presentation of it within your own being.

In a "live" class (as opposed to online, video, or text tutorials), the teacher, subject, and audience are present to one another at the same time. The richness of this "presence" has a great deal to do with the success of life-to-life transfer of what is *real*-ized in one person to others. The teacher orchestrates the movement, between himself and students, of teaching and response—connecting subject to student, drawing out and filling, providing practice with the language, logic, and skills of the subject. The process inevitably involves questions—a good teacher asks great questions, stimulates good questioning, and solicits even lame questions to get students

25 – Classes, Workshops, Seminars

engaged. The finest teaching is, really, a collaboration between an excellent teacher and people who are excellent at being taught.

Course design is a selection process informed by the teacher's passion, experience, education, philosophy, goals, and limitations. The scope and sequence, course outline, agenda, or syllabus that results—maps of this territory—reflects his creative resolution of constraining tensions such as lack of funds or space, student readiness level, and the place of this course within a larger program. Teaching is an art, like drama, and it requires some of the same performer and audience skills as a good play. A great chemist may not be a particularly good chemistry class designer. The English Literature class may look wonderful on paper, but the English teacher's lack of enthusiasm may sink it.

An excellent teacher may do a great job keeping one step ahead of the students in a textbook-based class if he is a quick learner and enjoys the role of tutor—facilitating students' understanding of an author-teacher's work. Indeed, some of the best teaching occurs when a bright, interested person serves as a role model in approaching a subject that is new both to him and to less advanced students. The presence of such an experienced learner helps awaken students' appetite for self-directed study. If a teacher is not able to be a beginner, a willing learner, in some sphere, his ability to connect with students in his own sphere of expertise will suffer.

Among all these components of a class, very few may be under your control. As a student, you may only rarely, if ever, experience an example of this form at its best. Nevertheless, you'll contribute to the improvement of your own experiences with classes if you a) are humble—willing to cede control of the form to a teacher or author for some time period and to accept the class from their hands; b) learn the new words necessary for intellectual understanding—dig, define, question to make sure your mind is engaged; and c) respond.

As with all forms, to make your experience as fully dimensional as possible, this three-step approach is invaluable. You will be applying your childlike docile presence, your youthful application to the effort of understanding, and your mature response-ability in your approach to form. You will bring the consciousness of expanding your own freedom, your own capacity for reality—and thus for

Christ—into every encounter with form. Too often, people sit under the teaching of another with a merely critical spirit—unable to respect the teacher's authority (limited, within this sphere) or enter into the experience as a participant in submission to its formal constraints. If they would someday try to teach, they might appreciate the form considerably more!

This attitude is shared by those who sit outside the Church, or outside community, looking in critically but refusing to enter into the smallness and struggle of actually experiencing the form from within. They apparently do not realize their stance—far from being godlike in its distance from the form they judge, it is actually childish in its attempt to reduce reality to their own dimensions. They may have come up against the challenge of entering this form through specific structures (enter the Church through RCIA; enter a building through doors; enter a class through prerequisites; enter a book through grammar; enter a foreign country through language study and guidebooks), and they interpret the difficulty as a message that they are not welcome here.

Though a class is a form, its teacher may have a more formal or less formal style. He may see his role as Facilitator, Coach, Lead Student, Socratic Questioner, Master of Ceremonies, or Expert Lecturer. Students will grow flexible—able to enter into various styles of teaching—as they encounter various expressions of the form. Teachers usually self-select what age level is best suited to their own style of pedagogy. Unfortunately, those who teach best the best-formed students find fewer and fewer students prepared to operate at that level, even in college. As with books, some classes will be, should be, intimidating to you. Don't let challenge stop you completely in your tracks; rather, consider whether you are ready and willing to meet this particular challenge.

Chess master and martial arts champion Josh Waitzkin, in *The Art of Learning*, mentions two different learning styles that result in two very different approaches to the difficulty of an encounter with new material. The "entity" learner tends to grasp new things in a "whole" (here, we might say "poetic") way but also to shut out anything that is not immediately accessible in this way. This person interprets the discomfort of failure as the sign that this new skill,

25 – Classes, Workshops, Seminars

subject, or form is simply not available to him. Alternatively, the "incremental" learner perceives failure as a sign that he has not put enough work into apprehension or practice, and he tends to overcome tremendous challenges in order to master and appropriate whatever he chooses. The great thing is, just by knowing that these two approaches are possible, you can learn to choose to not perceive challenge—in a class, a book, or another form—as a closed door!

26 – Gestures

WHEN YOU MAKE the sign of the cross, stand up to sing the national anthem, or go on a pilgrimage, you are entering into a "form" of sorts. Your gesture embodies—literally—values, truths, meaning in a powerfully effective, three-dimensional fashion. Formal courtesies and rituals can, of course, be executed in a flat, one-dimensional way. We say they are "meaningless," "mere formalities," or "empty gestures." To refill gestures with meaning is the work of maturity. A child might perform the gesture for fun, on command, or without concern for its meaning.

A young person might recognize hypocrisy or pointlessness and discard the gesture without realizing why it once was required or what he loses by tossing it too readily. When we have gestures-as-forms in our family, Church, or social culture, we also have anti-gestures. It's much easier to demonstrate contempt, for instance, by sitting out the Star-Spangled Banner in a culture where everyone else stands to honor the flag. If no one gets the gesture, the anti-gesture is impotent, too.

The story of Shadrach, Meshach, and Abednego—thrown into a fiery furnace for their refusal to bow to King Nebuchadnezzar's golden statue as to a god—illustrates the power of gesture to embody meaning. Gestures of courtesy—a man opening a door for a lady, a thank-you note, a response to the RSVP on an invitation—convey honor to others as we embody the principle of placing others above ourselves. In a culture with less and less commonality of meaning—shared languages, rituals and customs—the power of a gesture is compromised. We are aliens to one another. We exist in separate narratives, each self atomized and alone.

But we can, and should, reclaim the power of gestures, courtesies, rituals, and words! As Catholics, we are called to refill signs with meaning from the fountain of the wholly full Blessed Sacrament. We leave each Mass refilled with Christ, with meaning, with person-

26 – Gestures

hood, in order to rekindle sacred fire in every form, every vessel we can find. Much as the early Church refilled pagan gestures (feast days, sacred spaces, symbols such as trees and fire) with the superabundance of the Christ story, we can infuse our own real world with His light.

The traffic light will remind us of the Trinity. The celebration of Independence Day will become a prayer for the genuine human freedom of our leaders and fellow citizens. Gentlemen who stand when ladies enter make a silent, beautiful comment to all who observe. The customer who expresses gratitude for good service reminds the waiter or repairman of his human dignity and elevates their transaction into an opportunity for God's grace to touch another person. You may embody all the values you hold dear in small gestures like these. Others may or may not understand the significance or join you in performing them, but you will be lifted. You will be creating new vessels for grace with each attempt to *realize* value in form. Gestures have more power than most people understand.

When a whole series of gestures is prescribed on certain occasions, we have rite, or ritual—close kin to drama—in which words and movements of each person are choreographed into a formal "reenactment" of story. Rituals are suprapersonal, communal gestures—holding open the space between us so we can experience the embodied values as participants. Ritual embodies the relationship of self to others, to authority, and to a mission. The newcomer senses both the huge edifice of group identity and the open door of learnable gestures that signify and accomplish his incorporation. "We" re-present our narrative to remember who we are *and* to let "you" discover your place in our movement toward our destiny.

We can drain rituals of meaning by refusing to "act our part"— consider graduation ceremonies whose formalities are scoffed at and spoofed by childish participants, men who won't ask ladies to dance at a formal ball, and those who don't audibly utter the Creed or the responses at Mass. Rituals are natural to human beings—created to imbue significant events and transitions with meaning. From the Greeks' ceremonial recital of the Iliad to the Native Americans' manhood initiation rites, human beings are storytellers, ritual re-enactors, celebrants of transcendent values. Josef Pieper, in *Leisure, the Basis of Culture*, warned that false celebration and ritual would fill the void left by unbelief.

During the French Revolution, rituals of the Church were co-opted for service to the new regime. Ball game waves and cheers, sorority initiations, and prom traditions all unify participants in a sense of belonging that is less universal than that of the Church. The more distant a ritual from a basis in truth that includes all human beings, the more you should question what is embodied there, who chose its values and created its form, and whether you should participate. As with gestures, rites like these can mean different things to different people, and we must interest ourselves in the significance of this rite for the individuals who consider it meaningful.

Catholics are often accused of "putting on airs" and of rote compliance with traditional rites. If you don't understand the liturgy as a participation in a dramatic, ritual re-presentation of the Passion, you might think that your sitting, standing, responding, and singing are just so much empty form. While it may be true that "the show" will go on with or without you, something real is deleted from the form—it is less fully *real*-ized without your in-formed participation. Because it is, specifically, not a "show" for you to watch but a "living drama" for you to enter into and help enact, it invites you to an exercise of freedom that helps expand your interior freedom and response-ability.

An incorrect understanding of the liturgy as a form that the congregation creates is at the root of much of today's liturgical abuse. Though your free action contributes to its realization, the liturgy is God's own form, created by the Holy Spirit through the agency of the Church and enacted in continuity throughout two thousand years of its existence. The Mass is an experience that is celebrated continuously in a heavenly realm that we gain entrance to through the door of liturgy. *Leitourgia* is, literally, our portion of a greater, public and universal work. The Divine Office is another form of this great Work by which we gain entrance to a three-dimensional, living reality of presence in the full assembly of the faithful before God.

The high-sounding language of liturgy may seem snobbish or old-fashioned if you don't realize that it is meant not just to communicate information but also to help create an atmosphere of epic story, of drama. The language of liturgy invokes and celebrates our presence before the throne of God, where angels participate in the amazing and holy form. As C.S. Lewis points out in his *A Preface to Paradise Lost*, liturgical language is not meant to sound like the language of friends chatting casually together, a talk-show host going over today's program, or a hive of bees droning. That high language is indicative of the highest elevation of the human person, in the elevation of the highest Person ever known.

We have said that every form is an invitation to freedom. (Those who can hear, let them hear.) Form demands nothing yet invites the response—and thus the freedom—of recipients. The gesture may or may not be fully formed in those who receive it. (For instance, one who opens the door for a lady may give her the impression she has been demeaned, or treated with contempt. Her response to the form as it affects her is likely to be negative, though the gesture was intended to convey honor to her.) Because it is first formed in the person or persons who give it, nothing is lost to them (though they may feel disappointed) if no one can receive it, or if the recipients receive it only badly. To paraphrase G.K. Chesterton, a thing worth receiving is worth receiving even badly.

Father Luigi Giussani taught his students to respond to reality in gestures that embody their faith, their concern for the human person, their perspectives as college students, parents, and professionals, and the particulars of their circumstances. Attention to this crucial step in the educational process has resulted in position papers, brochures, posters, performances of music and drama, educational exhibits, panel discussion and speaker events, and humanitarian gestures of solidarity with those in need.

The annual meetings, in Rimini and New York, of the international Communion and Liberation community founded by Father Giussani—itself a gesture grown into an institution—brings together thousands of people who are learning to bring their faith and particular personhood to bear in responses to the unique situations they face at work, home, and school and in civic and religious communities. Each confrontation or encounter with reality can result in a response, a gesture, by which God, through our human freedom, turns even the most difficult challenge into an invitation to freedom that elevates and ennobles all concerned.

There are gestures we make as a family: all the doing-with-significance by which we embody our values, honor our loved ones, and retell our story in traditions serious and silly. Even the nightly bedtime ritual and the annual Hobbit party grow in power with every repetition. The gestures we carry out as the body of Christ are the making of us—truly knitting believers together one genuflection, one eucharistic procession, one service project at a time—and also the doorway into that body for whoever is watching and wants entrance. Groups of friends, like Communion and Liberation's Schools of Community, are formed and help form others through gestures as simple as one excellent question posed to invite reflection and response.

You can't make a list of good gestures and accomplish them all. You'll need a lifetime to appropriate the riches of the Mass. You can't possibly understand and respond to all the gestures performed by others. But the vastness of this territory should not prevent your exploration of it. To be more conscious that you are looking at, or into, a form is to be better able to enjoy whatever you can grasp of its fullness As Gerard Manley Hopkins wrote in *God's Grandeur*, "The world is charged with the grandeur of God. It will flame out, like shining from shook foil." As you help refill signs, this grandeur "gathers to a greatness" in the body of Christ, to reanimate the world.

27 – Dialogue

When you chat over coffee, you don't feel like you're creating a "form." In fact, it wouldn't be as enjoyable if it felt "formal." Formality implies stiffness, rules, boundaries, prescribed topics—exactly the opposite of the fun, freewheeling, spontaneous conversation you have with good friends.

In reality, though, you really are obeying rules, observing conventions, engaging in a form of interpersonal dance that fascinates scientists who watch slow-motion videos of unorchestrated conversations. Through courtesy and friendship emerges a form that enjoyably engages your freedom in a "bondage" you don't mind. The greater the mutual affection that participants feel, the more they are locked into attention to their conversation partner's movements, hesitations, nuances, and thoughts. You actually conform to one another, mirroring with complete un–self-consciousness the "other self" seen in a friend.

Not all dialogue is this easy. The less you trust the other, the fewer things you have in common, the less you look alike—the more you shut his image out of your heart, out of your movements and gestures. You are strangers, guarded and wary, and conversation, if it flows at all, reflects that alienation in every muscle of your bodies. More likely, it never even begins.

This dynamic is understandable, natural, even predictable. The problem is that when this behavior is multiplied throughout society, various people-groups grow further and further apart. In a vicious cycle—the less you talk, the less you want to talk—the distance seems greater, the barrier grows higher. Conservatives and liberals, Catholics and Protestants, Christians and atheists, Muslims and Hindus, men and women, working moms and homemaking moms, vegans and paleo dieters—it's uncomfortable to talk, so we don't.

As a corrective, think of dialogue as a form—one you can create with others who value brotherly love, or world peace, or a less ridiculously polarized social climate. Possibly the most important conversations in the world today are interfaith dialogues. Essential beliefs are the most personal and most difficult to discuss without triggering self-defense and deafness to one another.

The Catholic Church is a world leader in interfaith dialogue. But unless the message re-sounds through us, the Church's gesture will be emptied of power. Unless *my* heart is pierced, *my* tone of voice changed, *my* pride chastised, *my* lack of charity rebuked, *my* fears resolved, *my* family taught to respect the stranger in our midst, *my* world will not change. You and I are called to echo the message that peace is possible.

But we aren't sure what to say, how to say it, when to smooth over differences and when to address them. It's scary to approach people who have been caricatured for us by those who feed our fears and who feed on sensation, conflict, despair. We rarely are exposed to the intelligent conversation of those who respectfully disagree yet peacefully build unity upon shared values and shared humanity. People of faith are marginalized and demonized as irrelevant anachronisms and irrational fanatics. We are silenced by fear, confusion, and ignorance.

Our silence, our impotence does not serve to bring peace; does not contribute to the coming of the kingdom of love; does not protect us from evil. The Word of God—the Logos, the living and creative Word—is meant to be spoken. The truth that sets free, the message that conveys faith to its audience, the *re*-sounding, reverberating love of God is transmitted through human beings speaking together. We must speak, but with the voice of unity. Being right does not make us righteous. The time, patience, and humility we invest in building authentic human relationships give us our forum and our freedom to speak truth in love.

You must be unified—in the family, in your friendships and communities, in the Church—in order to speak as one with your neighbors. The Trinity teaches us to place the other person above self—a wisdom that is first of all pure and peace-loving. Christians are called to make manifest God's oneness by extending the kingdom of reconciling love to our neighbors for love of Him who has first loved us. The manifest unity of Christians is the Church—a

27 – Dialogue

pillar of fire shining in the world of darkness, shining for all to follow. The Church leads the international dialogue; the individual believer leads the local and more personal form.

The Church's position regarding your non-Catholic neighbor is clear. This person is first of all a human being, worthy of all dignity and loving protection by virtue of bearing the image of God as His beloved creature. He may be imperfect, wrong, or hard to get along with. Unity is not about our perfections or our uniformity but about God, who desires that we live in peace with one another. Unity cannot occur between ideologies, institutions, camps, or philosophies. Unity implies human beings in conversation.

Blessed Pope John Paul II said that it is "urgent for believers themselves to foster relations characterized by openness and trust, and leading to common concern for the well-being of the whole human family.... The name of the one God must become increasingly what it is: a name of peace and a summons to peace." Pope Benedict XVI said that interreligious dialogue "cannot be reduced to an optional extra. It is in fact a vital necessity, on which in large measure our future depends." Both popes perceive that the recapitulation of the human person and recognition of the centrality of the human person constitute the key to counteracting "the disruptive power of ideologies." You must be free and invite others to freedom!

Love, without which our best theology is empty of meaning, must be the basis of any attempt to build unity with our neighbor. To be one with the loving heart of God, you can do no better than follow Mary's example. From the Cross, Jesus left her to be the Mother of all the living—a new Eve to restore the brooding, hovering, creating, comforting, communicating love of the Holy Spirit to all the world's children. Just before Our Lord experienced the utter forsakenness of man alone and in need of a Savior, He gave her to the Church and abandoned Himself wholly unto death. Whenever Mary is seen or heard, she points to this moment of Christ's self-abandonment on the Cross as the key to unity with Him. The enemy sows fear. The mother sows love and teaches us to be unified to others in love.

You are a bridge between Christ and the person you encounter. Your genuine love speaks more truly about Him than all your words. In the encounter with your heart, your neighbor has an encounter with Christ that may be life changing, or it may not even be noticed. The perfect love from heaven moves through your heart to cast out their fears. Where there is not time to develop a deep relationship, your love must shine through token gestures of courtesy and simple human kindness. God's love must first cast fear out of your heart, and then you will not be afraid of the strangeness of your neighbor.

In your conversation, especially when you disagree, you demonstrate that your neighbor is deserving of dignity and respect not because he is on "your side" but because he is human. For a world that often seems to be losing its mind, Catholics can give the example of reasoned, logical, peaceful dialogue. The public nature of the Church's conversation helps reconcile others to accepting differences. Through Mary, the Holy Spirit is working in the world to draw all men to the Father through the Son. The body of the Son, His Church, is given to the world to bring all men into unity with the Prince of Peace.

There is a work in the Church called, officially, the Work of Mary. Less formally known as Focolare (Italian for "hearth of the home"), the movement's particular charism, its emphasis for our times, is the promotion of the deep unity among persons for which Christ allowed Himself to be utterly forsaken on the Cross. The amazing success of this work is just one example of the operation of the Spirit. There are now Anglicans, Jews, Buddhists, and Muslims learning from Catholic Focolare the way of love!

Chiara Lubich, Focolare's foundress, taught that willingness to participate in Christ's forsakenness on the Cross is the key to unity. What must you forsake in order to live in unity with your neighbor? Pride? Power? Indifference? Fear? Self-righteousness? Chiara said, "It is a matter of momentarily putting aside even the most beautiful and greatest things we have ... in order to be 'nothing' in front of the other person.... We put ourselves in an attitude of learning.... We enter their world, in some way we become inculturated in them and we are enriched.... Our complete openness and acceptance then predisposes the other person to listen to us.... Real, true, heart-felt fraternity is, in fact, the fruit of a love capable of making

27 – Dialogue

itself dialogue, relationship, that is, a love that, far from closing itself within its own boundaries, opens itself toward others and works together with all people of goodwill in order to build together unity and peace in the world."

The word "dialogue" (*dia*: through, *logos*: word) implies the piercing through of a person by words. Through dialogue, two hearts may be pierced by the living Word of God, the two-edged sword of Truth. Dialogue is a call to life—against violence; a call to faith—against fear; and a call to reason—against confusion. The Catholic–Muslim Forum and other interreligious initiatives are calling people of all faiths to stand together in unity under God and trust Him to make a "way in the wilderness" (Isaiah 43:19)—a way where there is no way—to unity. Catholics know the name of that Way, and we have a responsibility to learn to trust Him with our nothingness when we stand before the person who does not yet know Him. Blessed Pope John Paul called dialogue the "art of spiritual communication."

As a form, conversation seems flat or shallow when we merely repeat the same words back and forth to one another. A "two-dimensional" dialogue might introduce some struggle or tension; it requires more of your skill and interest and seems more like work. Dialogue as a three-dimensional form allows the Holy Spirit to quicken this tension into a new thing: a loving unity that embraces another person with such strength that you and he can find resolution and creative response in the midst of your words.

Remember that entrance into any form is a three-step process. First, allow yourself to be "nothing," to simply be present and be affected by the other person. Establish your unity and return to this basis of trust any time that unity seems threatened by the conversation. Next, move into the second dimension—defining terms and setting some boundaries to make clear what tensions this unity will be expected to bear. The phase of preparation for formal dialogues, debates, or panel discussions often takes much longer than the actual public conversation. Remember this when you feel impatient to begin. Even a private dialogue between strangers needs some formality and mutual agreement on the terms of engagement.

In dialogue, as we have seen with every form, the fullest realization, or dimensionality, is only possible through the action of the

Holy Spirit upon that natural, human gift you offer to Him. Do the best you can to be loving and respectful, but beg for His presence, His grace. Then, have the best conversation you can and watch what He does with it. When you experience real love, joy, and freedom in the interaction, you know that the miracle of Christ's coming upon and overshadowing natural elements has happened again! For you, this form has become a place of encounter with Christ.

28 – Institutions

G.K. Chesterton said, "All free men create institutions." Do you wonder what he meant, or why "free men" would do such a thing? When you realize that the institutions people create are forms that embody or structure their values, beliefs, and desires in such a way as to invite others "in" to experience them, it makes more sense. We've come to think of institutions as dead things in ugly buildings, but the ones created by free men are alive, variously shaped, and part of the infrastructure for truth, beauty, and goodness in this world.

Nonprofits and businesses, formal associations and informal clubs, ancient brotherhoods and children's museums all exist to conserve, hold, protect, and pass on something of value. If you look into them deeply, you find someone who sacrificed to extend something of personhood into the future. This side of heaven, man cannot transcend time except through his forms—his works of art, his books, his institutions. The fact that many of these creations are flat, ugly, even offensive shouldn't make us lose sight of the authentically human propensity to make more of them. The answer to ugliness is not to simply stop generating forms but rather to encourage people formed in faith and in beauty to generate more forms!

Joseph Putnam, in *Bowling Alone*, showed that the strength of society's "cultural capital" is directly related to the number, strength, and interconnectivity of its institutions. From book study groups and stitch 'n' sip clubs to the Heifer Project and the International Barbershop Harmony Society, free men create vessels for the collection, protection, and dissemination of whatever they consider valuable.

Through the institution of marriage, a couple's union is formalized, sacralized, given social standing as the *corpus* through which children will emerge and be nurtured. Certainly, valuable things happen outside institutions (plenty of art never makes it into a museum, for instance, and a great deal of education occurs outside the school building), but those things are more ephemeral and private. Life can be crushed out of such forms when their weight, inflexibility, cost, or infrastructure overwhelms mission, key relationships, or core values. Creation of institutions involves sacrifice—for instance, we trade intimacy with cofounders for wider participation, flexibility for public accountability, or low overhead for greater financial stability.

Because we suspect institutions of being cold, impersonal, and life-draining, we are tempted to dismantle or disregard them. Non-Catholics often say, "The authentic Church should be an organism, not an organization." But, as science readily demonstrates, there are no living organisms in existence that do not exhibit a breathtaking degree of organization. Truly, organization must be at the service of life, but as truly, life must be well organized in order to thrive.

Some institutions are given the force of law. Canon Law helps establish religious communities and protects the institution of marriage, for example. Corporate law enables an institution to act "as a person"—making promises, incurring obligations, earning income. Through institutional formation, we govern greater tension, extending the boundaries of self to take greater risks as a created, corporate "self." The new "person" must have identity—a narrative of origin and purpose—in order to grow on a secure foundation. Often, just as with individuals, growth exposes weaknesses that must be addressed. The further the "person" moves from origin, from core activities, from primary relationships, the stronger the identity must be. Reconnection with one's own history is often critical at this stage.

Also, as such a "person" grows, mission, goals, operational ways and means, and core values must be more and more fully developed and articulated. Reflection and self-evaluation must occur continuously. Change, as it happens, must be consciously integrated and consistent with the reality of the past. Without a "hermeneutic of continuity," "real" persons and "institutional" persons are in danger of destabilization and self-destruction.

The power of human institutions to leverage individual goodwill into more effective action is illustrated by private hospitals, Habitat for Humanity, Missionaries of Charity, and thousands of other

28 – Institutions

examples. People want to be part of something greater, especially when fighting against great odds. The history of monasticism's positive effects on the social, spiritual, economic, and cultural fabric of the Middle Ages is well known. What you want to think about is the commonalities between institutions-as-form and the other forms you explore. Each one illuminates the others, as various metaphors help illuminate aspects of a particular subject.

29 – Systems

A SYSTEM MAY BE the least human form that man can create. Because it involves layer upon layer of man-made structure, system formation involves more and more cost and inflexibility. The more layers, the more distance between system-control and the free action of human beings. For example, federal, state, and local governments hold open a giant gap between the president of the United States and the father of a family. The system is supposed to help them communicate effectively, to ensure that the higher person or institution serves the lower, and to protect the lower levels from the stronger upper levels that are more detached from the sphere of personal action and accountability. More often, the structures of the system get in the way, interfere with communication, and overburden the individuals or component parts.

Hospital systems own and govern large collections of hospitals—hopefully bringing best practices to all. Large school systems supplant locally controlled neighborhood schools with the goal of standardizing higher educational achievements across geographical regions. The banking system is, presumably, more stable than a local bank could be on its own. Every system is someone's answer to questions about human scale, subsidiarity, control. Each one is a resolution of tensions between efficiency and humanity, local and nonlocal interests, costs and benefits. You need to be able to examine those answers, those judgments, in light of what you know about the human person and in light of your own freedom.

We may wish that our systems—expensive and top-heavy as they tend to be—could be more like the systems of the body, which operate wonderfully well, with greater balance between whole and parts and with less cost and coercion. The man-made system, as it grows farther away from the origin of action in the freedom of individuals, tends to grow more costly and coercive the more components it holds in tension. As with a person, as tension between elements

29 – Systems

mounts, a system's self-defense mechanisms tend to favor the whole at growing cost to the parts. Systems exert more destructive control over noncompliant individuals as a person might ignore foot pain to finish a basketball game.

Inasmuch as a system—like a systematic theology or a legal system—embodies truth and rightly orders its components, it serves the best interests of the persons (and their institutions) that it exists to serve. A theology founded on heresy, a legal system based on rejection of God's—or natural—law, or a school system created to minimize parental influence over children cannot truly preserve doctrines, morals, or people. Because systems are distant from the sphere of personal action, removed from the influence of individuals, they are more stable and much harder to change.

We exert influence through our institutions, which collect and substantiate our judgments and choices. Without institutional aggregation of individual preferences, the structures of a system can and do begin to crush the persons within. The value of form is that it can embody, protect, and communicate what is true, good, and beautiful. The danger of form is that it can entrench and disseminate falsehood, evil, and ugliness instead. When error takes form, the reality of that form masks the error within, giving it presence and authority and therefore power to affect those who cannot discern what actually is embodied there. It is, thus, of tremendous importance to be growing up in all things—learning to evaluate the structures that mediate reality to you—as fully as possible.

The Church teaches us to evaluate systems based on how well they serve the best interests of their components without undermining the "whole." The Catholic principle of subsidiarity suggests that control be exerted at the lowest possible level to prevent the top-heaviness of more centralized control. The Catholic understanding of the human person suggests that a government system exists to serve persons, families, and human institutions (rather than to merely serve itself or to force them to serve the government).

If the doctrines and proof texts exist to prop up a "system of heretical theology"; if poor people become props for the existence of an entrenched class of social service workers; if human workers become props in an economic system—then free men and women, acting in solidarity, will be needed to dismantle that system. In fact, unless a system corresponds to the reality of human freedom, it is doomed to fail, no matter how powerful it seems. Where is slavery or communism now?

As Catholics, we may worry about the systems, the many forms, that are arrayed against the Church, against truth, goodness, and beauty, against families, against virtue, but such forms must not be the lens we look through. By definition—embodying the denial of Truth—they are lies and cannot mediate reality to us. We must train ourselves, our children, and our students to see truly by seeing through forms that correspond to reality, to Truth, to the Real Presence. Once you realize you are always seeing reality through some form, influenced by form, then you realize that you must *choose* to see truly. Does this sound like advice to put on rose-colored glasses, or blinders? Nothing is further from my intention. To see truly is to see through the reality that Christ has won the victory. Pessimism likes to dress up as realism, but it doesn't correspond to the fullness of reality.

Engineers are trained to look for a certain quality in systems they design that indicates delicate balance and effective efficiency. "Elegance" is a beautifully simple solution to a complex problem, and it enables more to be achieved with less structure. According to Matthew May, in *Pursuit of Elegance*, elegance involves doing more with less, adding value by subtracting unnecessary and burdensome elements, and providing for the sustainability of the solution or process. Elegance has to do with beauty, symmetry, scale, proportion, and harmony, but those who use this language are rarely speaking from a religious point of view.

Since beauty is a transcendent value, however, the Catholic person speaks this language! What mathematicians look for in systems of equations and what physicists seek in systems of subatomic particles, you can seek in other forms. Dialogue, economic models, maps, paintings, novels, sonatas, a pilgrimage, or a business can incorporate and be improved by elegance as a design principle. There is a simplicity that precedes complexity, and a simplicity—elegance—on the far side of complexity. Maybe you can improve the systems that serve you by helping to pare them down

29 – Systems

to the least-possible structure serving the greatest-possible human need.

Art may be the first thing you think of when I propose that form is an embodiment of its maker's values and experiences. The more you understand about forms, in general, as structures created to mediate reality to some audience, the better you understand the capacity of art—whether music, drama, painting, poetry, literature, architecture, or sculpture—to be a *place* where Christ may be encountered. In the midst of an encounter between artist and audience, or simply between an individual and a work of art, the Holy Spirit often breathes life into a word or image that speaks to the soul.

Everything you learn about form in-*forms* your approach to art. Your encounters with art, conversely, have the potential for expanding your capacity to appropriate the wealth stored in other forms. We have to ask why, if art has such power to link man's heart to the fulfillment of all his desires, does art seem to accomplish so little evangelization or strengthening of weak faith.

Much of the "art" you see or hear seems more de-formational, more like the anti-gesture of negation of Truth and of God's presence. Some of it is overtly anti-Catholic (for example, horribly desecrated images of the Virgin Mary), but much more argues against the inherent dignity of the human person, the design of God for marriage, the possibility of man's correspondence to reality, and other principles of human *being* that Catholics consider essential to human welfare.

Not everything called "art" is, obviously, art's highest exemplar. There are very different thought systems, mental maps, or lenses generating confusion in creating, evaluating, and understanding art. For some, art is an almost magical emergence from within the mystery of the artist, subject to no external laws, judgments, or constraints. For others, art is a vehicle used to express or a vessel laden with the artist's emotions, beliefs, experiences, or personality. The Catholic sense of art—a via media between the extremes of modernity's artist-as-demigod and an iconoclastic rejection of art as sub-spiritual—maintains the personhood of the artist in the context of a preeminent Creator and affirms the value of even imperfect attempts to represent reality through works of art.

Beauty is a critical aspect of the environment, the context of being that may be overlooked when more pressing, pragmatic concerns overwhelm man. Art is important in the lives of human beings—for resolution of tension, for self-expression, for skill-building, for justice, and for humanizing and beautifying the fallen world. Those who consider art instruction superfluous do not realize that its very nature is ordered to superfluity: the nonfunctional, gratuitous beauty that God supplied for the sake of His own joy in giving it and to call man beyond necessity and function to a destiny in the heart of Beauty. Like philosophy, art cannot be valued except in light of its transcendent purposes.

Dorothy Sayers, in *The Mind of the Maker*, explores the threefold structure of artistic work—idea, action, effect—and suggests that our experiences of trying to create a work of art help illuminate the Trinity. Just as the metaphors "father," "lion," "physician," and "judge" help us understand some aspects of God's being, the metaphor "artist, or creator" is a rich source of insight.

The trouble is that so few people have much experience as creators. Fewer still will call themselves "artistic" or "creative" (even when they *are!*)—leaving those attributes to "professionals." Still, by learning to appreciate art, speak its language, and enter its forms with receptivity, anyone can appropriate some of its wealth. You also grow in understanding yourself—as a work of art, as an amateur artist, as the craftsman of your own life. Most people wrongly assume that to be creative is to issue forth in poetry, musical composition, sculpture—some form they recognize as a work of art. But true creativity springs up in every human response and is expressed in forms as diverse as philanthropy, engineering, and homemaking.

Leaving the struggle to be creative—to realize one's ideas in form—to a future book, let's look at how to become a better receiver of the gift of self that is art. Art is a turning point where the artist's response-in-form to the realities he encounters becomes a gift of himself to you. As you have seen, every response can become a gift, a movement back to God, through being freely given. If it then effects, or moves the recipient to, a response, you could say it is finally fulfilled. Except that, for the most powerful gifts, the movement keeps going. The repercussions of one gesture, one poem, one

29 – Systems

story can go far beyond the person of its creator into the future and into other persons and their works.

Human persons have being in the forms they create and in those who receive those forms. Dorothy Sayers said, "A great poem like Dante's *Divine Comedy* comes to us now enriched not only with all those events and associations of the past out of which the poet fashioned his image, but also with the accreted events and associations of the six hundred years of his future and our past which lie between us and him." Through the arts we transcend time, in a sense, and one work links us to an entire lineage in continuity.

When you receive well (and who among us can receive smallest fraction even passably well?), you enter a world of sorts, a world whose every artifact points back to the artist. The veil between you and the artist is sometimes more transparent, sometimes less. Scholars still argue about Shakespeare's identity, but G.K. Chesterton is almost palpably present as you read his writings. As with every form, you'll miss a great deal if you stomp in only to demand that the author come out and declare himself!

First, be simply present to the gift as given. Take time just to look at the painting, to read the story as a story (and not as the source for fill-in-the-blank answers about plot, setting, and character), to walk around inside the building. If it is detective fiction, you must take it on those terms and not judge it by the conventions of mythology or journalism. If it is liturgical music, you must consider its high purpose and not complain that it's not about you and your daily experiences. If it is an altarpiece, consider it in the context of the space it was designed to occupy (even if it is now hanging in a gallery).

If you refuse to experience a work of art poetically, wholly, and then push right into the territory of analysis and criticism, you will only receive a two-dimensional mental construct of the gift. Three-dimensional experience is predicated on the movement through the two prior modes of knowing. What can be said of art is doubly true for presuming to know the mystery of a human being. Maturation in the approach to one form increases your capacity to receive the other.

Those, for instance, who evaluate literature on the basis of what it accomplishes are likely to evaluate persons in the same utilitarian way. Catholic novelist Flannery O'Connor speaks powerfully, in *Mystery and Manners*, about the tendency of poorly formed readers to prefer propaganda to art in literature. The narrow-minded lack the self-confidence, the interior freedom, to enter form on its own terms, and thus they go about deriding forms that look suspiciously different from the cardboard-cutout mental models that inform their perceptions.

It is possible and necessary to criticize art (or any form) well. Without movement toward evaluation, you cannot make the informed judgment that leads to response, and thus to freedom. That evaluation, however, must take into account your own capability. For example, it is perfectly acceptable to say, "I have an aversion to that painting, but since I am in no way trained to struggle deeper into its meaning and quality, I can only respond to it as a child." Too often, receivers of the gift of art feel they must immediately pass judgment, whatever their qualifications to do so.

Art forms are vaguely threatening to those who are not comfortable in that foreign territory of symbolism, line, shape, proportion, harmony, material skill, historicity, and freedom. The power of beauty to, as Pope Benedict XVI has said, "wound" the recipient—to affect him, unbalance and disturb him—is both its threat and its promise to us. Not everyone is called to become an art critic; rather, we are called simply to know the limits of our authority to render judgment. The giving of a gift is the occasion not for a critique but for receptivity.

At the opposite extreme are those who consider a work of art immune to evaluation and critical judgment. The Catholic belief that beauty is not any more relative than truth—that it is possible to say something does or does not possess the qualities of beauty—is anathema to many in the world of art today. It implies that an artist has a responsibility not only to express his inner vision and practice his craft but also to communicate what is objectively true, good, and beautiful through his work.

G.K. Chesterton—for all his erudition and maturity—received created forms "as a child." He delighted in things as a child delights in a house of secret rooms, talking paintings, treasure chests, and passages to other worlds. This seeing truly, or realization, of reality

29 – Systems

is, to Chesterton, a religion, an adventure, an interior capacity he heartily wishes that every man could experience. His character in *Manalive*, Innocent Smith, approaches life as Chesterton did—with an informed innocence that brings new light into every situation through a man who seems to see the world upside down. We Catholics would say, rather, "right-side up"! Another Chesterton character, Gabriel Gale, is a poet with a similar in-sight that enables him to solve mysteries.

Chesterton had opinions about art, as about everything else, speaking not as an expert in a particular field but as one with this capacity to encounter reality whole and to make it his own. About art, then, he spoke not as a professor or art critic (though he had formal art training, sketched and painted, and wrote poetry, fiction, plays, and literary criticism) but as an amateur—that is, as a lover of the reality that caught his eye and his imagination. Everything he believed about art seems to come from this lived, experiential understanding, and not from a disembodied intellectual apprehension—much less from a snobbish or humorless elevation of art over lesser things. Art is *made* of "lesser things," is embodied in real men, leads to rock-solid dogma, and flows through the real world calling men to—never away from—beer, babies, home, and freedom.

Art, he said, is the "signature of man," setting him apart from animals. Art is born "when the temporary touches the eternal." "To awaken wonder . . . is the highest kind of art." Art is man's joyous response to beauty. Artists weave persons together in community. Artists reframe reality so that others can be awakened to wonder—stood on their heads to see the world aright. Even a list, Chesterton thought, could be a poem, and a lampstand—to a person with eyes to see it—an icon of all that is worth living and dying for.

The "man fully alive," in Chesterton's mind, is an Everyman who responds to reality as an artist—open to encounter, able to be affected and to respond, willing to give himself sacrificially in order to share his experience with others—all for the glory of God. The artist is not a superman but a child given the keys to a kingdom.

According to St. John Damascene, it is man's destiny, as icon of the divine mind, to "icon paint" the world—to restore it by realizing it fully, truly, intimately, within his own being. Sinful, fallen from his high calling, he waited in darkness for light to shine again into him through all things. Christ's coming relit the interior lamp, opened the inner eye again to the light from beyond this world that shines through trees, babies, grapes, and lampposts.

Blessed Pope John Paul called you to become an artist, crafting your own life as a work of art. If the living flame of the Holy Spirit is quickened in you, surely you will radiate that truth out into the world as, in unity with Christ, you respond to its beauties, restore its proportions, protect its harmonies, and integrate all its treasures into a hymn of praise. Truly did St. Irenaeus say, "The glory of God is man fully alive."

30 – The Church

THE CHURCH is "form" as a cathedral, as an institution, as a system of governed-together components, as a work of the Master Artist, as a person—the very body of Christ we believers are becoming—and as a community. In its gestures and rituals there are forms within forms—all educating, forming, cultivating the individuals who enter. The liturgy of the Church is her primary educational strategy—re-presenting, as it does, in *actuality*, the Body, Blood, Soul, and Divinity of our Savior. In its Scriptures we have a story and in its Divine Office a continual prayer that knit us together across time and space. In its Catechism the Church is present in the form of a book, or a class. The Our Father, or Lord's Prayer, is one of many examples of a structured approach to God, given to allow access to a disproportionate greatness.

You might say that Christianity is the most fully *formed* religion in the world, following the pattern of the Incarnation of its Founder. The full transparency that results is both its vulnerability and its strength. Form exposes values, intentions, presuppositions, and arguments to view. It is subject to scrutiny and criticism, misunderstanding and rejection. When we have the courage to *real*-ize, to embody and offer what we believe, we participate in a particular way in the crucifixion of Christ. Just as we are not "souls in body suits," the Church is not a purely spiritual reality. Her structures and forms are as intrinsic to her being as your nose is to yours! Let others keep their disembodied religions and abstract ethical systems. Catholics will choose the three-dimensional approach that corresponds more fully to reality and thus has more power to cultivate our freedom.

In the fullness of her being, the Church protects your being. Her architectural forms hold space open, inviting you to exit freely from the world of self to the worship of God. Her legal systems protect and coordinate your institutions—your marriage, your lay association, your local church. As an institution, she conserves the arts, channels charitable donations, voices the concerns of millions to their political leaders, educates the generations, and transmits pure doctrine. As a work of art, the Church shines with integrity, harmonious proportion, and clarity: the radiance of transcendent beauty. As a person, the Church models the works of mercy and incorporates the principles of subsidiarity and justice within her giving and serving structures. In this form, God has provided the perfect infrastructure to support the complexities of human development.

The imagery of one, two, and three dimensions does not indicate a stepwise ascent to a place of elite inclusion or esoteric knowledge; rather, it helps us see the movement from the first conception of a living thing or a created form to its fullest fulfillment. The Church, unique among all forms, is both a living being, created by God, and a collaboration with man in the creation of form. Here, we are affirmed in the slow, organic growth of persons into maturity. Here, also, we have a model for the action of the Holy Spirit upon the receptive mind of man in cocreation.

The work of creating art, institutions, and—to a lesser degree—other forms requires us to resolve this same tension between intrinsic "life" and imposition of mind in form. A novelist must be sensitive to the authentic development of his characters. A nonprofit organization must protect its fundamental mission from the very structures necessary to the accomplishment of that mission. If the greatest form is a creative resolution of the greatest tension, then the Church may well rank as the single highest form in existence. Only the life of a human being—crafted, like a work of art, in collaboration with God—approaches the greatness of the growing *real*-ization of Christ within the Church. She is the womb, the *matrix*, for His becoming, and she models the receptivity and courage we need to become artists or parents.

For parents and would-be educators, Mother Church is an excellent role model. For two thousand years she has, as we must do, created external forms, requirements and structures designed to call forth and support the life of her children's souls and their growth in Christ-likeness. She has handled the tension we feel as we hold the highest ideals and standards the world has ever known yet at the

30 – The Church

same time are responsible for leading to them the little, the weak, and the ignorant ones of the world. As with every kind of form, her very *actuality* will seem to some to shut them out. This is not an argument *against* form but *for* evangelization, teaching, and loving dialogue.

Within her family, as in ours, there has always been a diversity of strengths and capabilities. Her rules had to be consistent for all and yet also leave room for judgment—consideration of the context of an individual member's actions and his special needs. Mother Church has creatively and practically dealt with the paradox between what must be done for the physical, environmental, or temporal needs of her children and what can only be done for them by Christ. The Church has had to develop and change systems and approaches over time—learning from her mistakes and acknowledging herself in constant need of prayer and of God's grace.

Mother Church prays for herself and for her children. She prays constantly, systematically, specifically, and formally. She is under no illusion that she can exist in her own strength; rather, she has a system in place to make sure that daily prayers are offered for the practical and spiritual needs of her family. She uses formal language in prayer to draw her children in reverence toward the beauty of communication with God and to remind them that their destiny lies beyond this world. She prays even for those hostile to her, and for the peace of the territories in which she dwells. Rather than fearing the world around her, she engages it creatively and blesses the desert with the waters of mercy.

The Church is both "process" and "person" oriented. Process is the bridge between vision and manifestation, between the ethereal and the nitty-gritty, the ideal and the real. Principles must be given active vehicles for their outworking. It is not enough for us to love the Lord—we are required to come and worship Him. This obligation ennobles you and impels you to do the right thing when your resolve might be weak; it is hardly necessary otherwise.

Mother looks beyond her children to the next generations. She realizes that much of what she will do in their lifetime is plant seeds that will grow within their families far into the future. In this light, there is no cutoff age at which it is no longer worthwhile to improve family life, work on development of virtue, or restore broken relationships. She creates a rich culture and heritage over time, willing to invest for long-term gains. Without this perspective you can become mired in the "terrible *daily*-ness" of life—chafing at necessary routine and repetition. You can become driven by the tyranny of the urgent or seduced by promises of immediate gratification. A sense of the generations to come and of eternity orders your priorities toward lasting value, mortification of desire, "filling" time rather than "killing" it.

The traditions and practices of the Church and of families develop and change over time. Some things need time and adjustments to grow on us and feel authentic, to fit into the spaces of our lives where eternity and time intersect. As the sense of sacred time begins to overlay and infuse into the life of the family, our awareness of the profound significance of the Incarnation is heightened. The highest form within the Church's multilayered embodiment of Christ is the liturgy. As the form within which Christ and Church are one-d, the liturgy is both prerequisite and goal—source and summit—of the Catholic Faith.

Though human beings, with their flaws and sins, their ineptitude and mixed motives, have formed the Church, they've worked under the constant guidance of the Holy Spirit. Think of the Church as a created form, crafted to represent the resolutions of millions of Christians over thousands of years to hundreds of tensions common to human experience. You may benefit from her experience as you confront those tensions yourself. Think of the Church as, also, a person, growing up over time. Just like you, she's grown more and more able to resolve tension creatively, to take on other forms with skill, to articulate and formulate her boundaries and supporting structures, and to offer authentic response to lived encounter with the realities she has faced.

Through her support of an array of religious charisms, the Church embodies a creative unity-in-diversity that is an antidote to both diversity that fractures the whole and unity that smothers its own components or individuals. She affirms the possibility that the Holy Spirit can work through unique, unrepeatable persons in gestures that respond to a seemingly infinite variety of needs and circumstances. In organizations with smaller scope, there is often tremendous pressure toward homogeneity among the members. They cannot bear the tension of diversity, conflict, or community.

The perspective of eternity and the scope of universality permit the Church to embrace much greater tension and wait longer for its creative resolution. This is a pattern for anyone to follow: articulate the tension as fully as possible—struggle, work to be present to it, include all aspects of the reality you face, including your own interior response—and then be still, and wait upon the Lord to "develop the interference pattern" (see the section on holograms) and quicken into life a "new thing" that takes all of it into account, enables you to make a clear judgment, and becomes your fitting response.

31 – Community

THE WORD "community" is used in many different ways. It may mean "the town you live in" and be so large and vague that you cannot name all the individuals in your community. You may not even use the term for your most intimate associations with others—"family," "gang," "circle," "team," or "book group" seems more personal. Whatever human communities you belong to you probably didn't create. You simply found yourself in a family, gravitated naturally to the clubs and associations that correspond to your interests, joined others to work for common causes, or chose a church because of the vibrant community that already seemed to be active there.

But "community" can also be thought of as a created form—an embodiment of its founders' values, a fruit of someone's struggles to work out tensions, an invitation to live in some degree of commonality and unity with a particular group of other people. As a structure, a community may be more or less well-articulated (more "formal" or "casual," less "self-conscious," more "organic"). Religious communities are quite formal, as is the path to joining such communities. Lay associations of the faithful are encouraged and guided in their formation by the rules and procedures of the Church.

"Community" carries emotional associations. You may not feel that true community exists unless you have some degree of private or informal or personal association with others in your parish, or with your coworkers. On the other hand, you may be content to be "in community" with all other Catholics without spending time with them as individuals. For some, the word is reserved for those who have made a promise to live in unity, have taken vows to live together, or are in some way obligated to work through the inevitable tensions of coexistence.

The levels of commitment, of intimacy, of personal involvement, and of shared goals or values all contribute to the sense of "commu-

31 – Community

nity." For the purposes of considering community as created form, you can think of any examples of persons consciously set apart from others such that they live in a unity that requires them to work through practical, interpersonal, and spiritual tensions in order to maintain their association. The collaboration of persons to embody their interests and values by obligating themselves to one another to some degree results in a form that, ideally, invites others to share those foundational principles, but which also seems to exclude those others.

Within any community, there is pressure toward group norms, whether or not they are essential to the group's initial sense of itself. Ironically, there is a tendency toward this homogeneity as much within groups that place the individual above community—for example, within Protestant churches—as within communities like a communist country, where the individual is merely a building block for the bigger form.

The Catholic Church is ordered, as always, to the "both-and" response instead of an "either-or" polarization: the community or whole has priority *in order to* protect the individual's freedom to be truly and fully himself. Rituals, formal prayers, and traditions all contribute to the formation of Catholic community, manifesting the relationship of God to the Church so that individuals mature into their own God-and-I relationship.

Where the emphasis is first on an individual's personal relationship with God, the group is actually threatened from within, by its own nature, and unspoken pressure results in maintaining group conformity to reduce this tension. Where external, public behaviors are regulated and shared, there is actually more scope for the quirks of individual behavior. Where the group has an actual unity and identity, there is an organic infrastructure of support for the individual within it.

This has implications for family life—a small but critically important form of community. Is the individual the building block of the whole, or does the whole exist to serve its members? Because the protection of the "least among us" is the measure of the effectiveness of communities and institutions, they cannot succeed if they violate him. When building up the community becomes the measure of a person's worth, he is violated in that he is treated as a means to an end—a human resource.

Parents can find themselves focusing almost exclusively on their children's external, behavioral issues, to the exclusion of internal change and growth. They can be threatened by the uniqueness of the individual family member even more when society pressures children to rebel against every limitation imposed at home. If we, like the Church, stressed community-building (shared ritual, traditions, essential doctrines, formal prayer), entrusting individual growth to God within this strong context, we might not feel so pressured. Can you make "Catholic life" the focus of your family's life in community? Can you consciously create community with others in order to strengthen the context for your child's formation?

Catholicism provides a holy framework and unapologetically requires conformity of thought (doctrine) and practice (worship), not to make everyone a nonthreatening copy of everyone else but rather to give everyone the highest possible chance of becoming conformed—not to the pattern of this world, but to the mind of Christ. If my family holds out its individual identity as the first priority, the church or school we "create" will merely reflect our family "style," just as churches reflect the group personality of the individuals who gather together (attracted to one another as much as to Christ). Some are offended by the Catholic premise that the family is not given all the resources it needs to carry out its mission and must depend upon the Church to sustain it. This is not a weakened notion of family but simply a true one.

Within the context of Church, though, we may—and probably need to—form more or less formal communities, at least to make up for the lack of extended family that marks these mobile times. Education is often the focus of our attempts to find the help we need to raise our families. When parents get together, hoping for a school or education co-op to be formed, they sometimes have only vague ideas about the place of this new community in the context of Church and family.

They may reject the idea that this should be a community at all, preferring a more detached, institutional form for their school. The community form implies more personal involvement and so is usu-

31 – Community

ally the choice when there is less money available to hire employees. Both are legitimate forms for schools, and all schools are both "institutional" and "communitarian" to some degree. But it is problematic to jump in and generate form without clearly understanding the grammar, the dynamics, the materials, the limitations of that form. A period of questioning, examination of the realities you face, and articulation of a response based on "judgment with a heartbeat" is so important at this point.

If you simply copy secular schools, you run the danger of embodying formally some unexamined presuppositions and values. If you don't examine the cultural expectation that families are mere collections of individuals, you may undermine the family's own "community life" for the sake of the new educational institution. Without reflection on the goals you hope to accomplish for the children, you may focus, by default, on cranking out "good citizens," "good workers," or "kids who fit into society"—rather than free human beings.

True community is a hard thing to create. You'll need the help of the Holy Spirit to articulate your yearning for it, the boundaries and limitations you need respected, and the extent to which you can lay down your own individual life in order to contribute. And all that is just the first layer of complexity. After that, you must find others who want something similar and are willing (and able) to work together through the tensions of designing and building this new form. You might find that there already is a form you may join, to save you much of this trouble. This is why "free men always create institutions": so that every newcomer doesn't have to reinvent the wheel. Even when you join an ongoing group, there will be tensions to work through.

So far, you've perhaps created a new institution, but what will make it a community? Without a shared life, unity, some commitment, love, you don't have community. These things are harder to articulate, because they flow from the heart, unlike the bylaws and operational details that the intellect may have handled on its own. This is why "community" is a higher, harder thing: because so much of what is necessary here cannot be provided except by the freewill, mature engagement of persons. The Church has grown into her own being, struggling at first as any new community must with issues of personal vs. corporate interest, self-articulation, internal consistency, and more. It would be an extremely onerous thing for any of us to have to re-create the Church from scratch!

The issues facing a community are very personal, so emotional reality plays a role in its formation. Like a person, any institution has an "interior" and "exterior" dimension—its sustaining mission and philosophy, and its infrastructure and concrete organization. A corporation, club, or charitable organization is more like an individual in its "personhood," while a community is more like a family. This distinction is my own and is used more to help understand the dynamics of interpersonal relationships than to categorize groups one way or the other.

You can't wish away the fact that interpersonal dynamics will bring in uncontrollable, wild-card elements that make a community possibly the very hardest form to create. There is no way to get so "objective" that all the messy reality disappears. But reality is good! If you can offer all of it to the Holy Spirit, He will make something amazing that mere wood or paint or words could never become. The form of community, holding in tension as it does free human beings, can be a unity that communicates the Person of Christ to the world in a powerful way.

To see a new school as the goal, and the time of working closely with others as the means to achieve that goal, is one thing. To see the formation of a community as the goal, and the creation of a school as the unitive focus, is another. To see school as a place where someone readies the kids for college entrance exams results in one form. To frame it as a place where kids are taught the Faith, another. All these perspectives are legitimate, but they result in different questions, choices, and forms. When the designers/creators of a "new thing" are unconscious unaware of how different their perspectives might be, the community suffers from lack of clarity.

There is one huge difference between any form of Catholic education and most of "the world's" forms. The anti-Catholic, dominant cultural view is that education is a kind of forward progress forward in the evolution of an individual that occurs in a fairly straight line from birth to adulthood, or to whatever one's view of enlightenment is. In contrast, our Catholic view of the human per-

31 – Community

son shows us a growth that keeps spiraling back to integrate, and then forward to incorporate, whatever reality is encountered.

We want not a "finished adult" from our process but a fully realized person whose being—child/adolescent/adult—is integrated in support of his freedom. We want not a person whose mind is filled with one-dimensional knowledge bits but a person in whom the capacity for reality in its fullness has been formed. Man is meant—designed—to be *capax omnium*: to have the capacity to take in all of reality. The capacity grows with direct experience, with the exercise of intellect, and with actions and responses that become securely hardwired values.

These ways of encountering reality correspond to the frames, tensions, and forms in this book. They can be thought of as three "databases" that fill gradually over a lifetime. In a continual movement forward and back, you gradually move from "building the house" by wisdom, to its establishment in understanding, to filling it "with treasures" as you become what Adam was meant to be—the knower and realizer of all created being.

First is the database of experience, physical being, simple presence to reality through the senses; second, the database of words and the faculties of the intellect; third, the database of responses, habits, incorporated values, and virtues. As you grow up, you move toward group structures, toward judgment, and toward freedom without moving away from the self, from your own feelings, or from the need for childlike obedience.

When you perceive education as the formation of this capacity, as the development of these richly supportive databases, as the cooperation with the natural inclination toward freedom, then you see that you cannot possibly be in charge of "completing" a human person or even of designing an educational model that is perfect for everyone at every stage. You really are under less pressure, freed by the reality that formal education is, like the small spectrum of visible light, an important but narrow slice of education in its fullness.

Father Luigi Giussani taught that the "I" begins and develops from the point of contact with reality. It might seem like a no-brainer to keep your children in touch with reality, but the boundary of "what is real" becomes less and less clear as technology enables us more and more to escape physical reality and to "realize" even the wildest imaginations to some extent. Reality can end up being a small part of our lived experience, or we may experience only a very narrow slice of reality.

The "I," the human person, suffers from this—a reduction of being, of capacity for what is and thus for the great I Am. Many young people with identity crises are, in fact, suffering from reality deprivation. More and more, the sense of a self, with a past and a future destiny, and that coheres or hangs together over time, is disintegrating in the people around us. The weak "self" is easy prey for manipulators and destroyers, so the work of education and formation is a very serious business. If you can muster the courage to create a Catholic educational structure with some degree of community formation among the families, you will be fighting against the disintegration of the world!

You and your children will achieve different degrees of freedom within every different aspect of your education, but your interior freedom will grow steadily whatever material (a skill, a subject, a journey, an encounter with art, relationships, etc.) you work on. You'll want the child to be formed through encounter with reality and not to merely accomplish work.

Disconnected intellectualization of education can be caused by a method that generates linear progress but involves no engagement of the person's own heart. Father Giussani speaks of the "risk" of education. We present truths to our students and ask them to understand, be affected by, and respond—a cycle that helps them possess the truth in a fully engaged way, but which involves the risk that their encounter with truth will not affect them the way we hoped or that they will make a different judgment than we did. A truly Catholic education invites them to create their own freedom by freely affirming the "Catholic proposal" with a response based on a judgment that involves the "beat of the heart." How important it is, then, to cultivate a heart that responds to beauty, truth, and goodness—not just an intellect that casually affirms a code of ethics but cannot realize those values in action. You've got to want your children free, not just tame!

All the questions I raised in Tensions must be addressed, first by

31 – Community

individuals and then together in the formation of this new, community "self." Everyone involved brings the reality of their own being, their own skill set, their own expectations and hopes, and their own goals to the table. None of this can be ignored. The result won't completely please anyone, yet it must be more than just a pragmatic compromise. Ideally, the Holy Spirit will be invited to weigh in, helping you to resolve the tensions creatively, in ways that honor each person's reality. More likely, most of this work of self-examination, parent education, and clear articulation won't be done, and the problems this creates will just be addressed as they occur.

There is something to be said for this as a method: "let's just jump in together and work out problems along the way." You certainly can't plan in advance for every exigency, so why not meet problems as they spring up rather than try to plan them away. You wouldn't want to walk into a building built this way, but a lot of people go ahead and create communities, associations, and schools in similar fashion. The tensions are resolved and masked, to some extent, by the reality of the "new thing." Opportunity cost and future costs are invisible, so they are easily overlooked. What people do not, or cannot, say is also more difficult to take into account.

Like a monastic community, the new Catholic community needs a "rule of life"—an articulation of what is expected from each member, and why. The further you move from your origin in close relationships and shared understanding, the greater the need for articulation of your story, your operating principles, your reasons for the decisions now encased in form, and the path to involvement for newcomers. The larger the community grows, the less change will be possible, but there must be a way for members to contribute their judgments, ask for reevaluation, and continue to create the form.

A living form cannot be impervious to or over-susceptible to change. The more it is like a person, the more it will move through the same stages of growth that a person experiences. There is no return to origin, no stasis, and no infinite progress possible. There will be growing pains. The movement from simply being-me to communicating-me is challenging for individuals, institutions, and communities. Something is lost and something is gained as ideas are realized.

It is possible to face these challenges in a conscious, proactive way. This is what it means to cooperate in your own formation. This conscious identification of the community with a person allows you to see what stages you are in and are moving through, where your weaknesses and strengths are, and how you can bring the highest help into the process by inviting Christ into your individual judgments and responses. You need words—not empty slogans and vague, high-sounding phrases but solid words full of meaning and power—to generate a structure with integrity and the possibility for coherent growth.

We generally receive no formal training for creating community. You might want to practice on something smaller than creating a school together. You could form a Community 101 class with other parents. Start with a book study, move up to teaching one another whatever you know well, try designing a gesture together in response to something you've learned, travel together, create a service project, pool contributions for some financial need. Choose different people to lead these practices. Reflect on what works, what hurts, what you hated, and what you enjoyed. Learn to hear one another and to give your response as a gift. Then create a school together!

32 – The Human Person

THIS BOOK has been about the education and formation of the human person. If you respond, it becomes a book about you. I close, as I opened, with "person"—knowing I've not done full justice to Blessed Pope John Paul's call to "recapitulate the human person." The human person is the highest "form"—created by God but realized through the crafting of your own life.

All Creation seems anthropocentric and has waited, groaning, for the rebirth of its steward. In Christ, *person* is shown to be the key to the coming of the kingdom of God, the pivot point of the re-turned world, the tiny reality through which all Reality is to be realized and restored—its broken vessel mended and filled. In Mary, person is shown to be place: place for the indwelling Christ, place for others to encounter Him, place for hospitality and welcome to His banquet, place for the becoming of other persons. To say "place" is to say "three-dimensional." You have an interior dimension within which reality can have being.

A person is a microcosm of the world—a model for understanding and a lens for seeing it clearly. A person's life is a journey, an open book presenting his arguments to the world, a Life 101 course where others may learn from his experience. A human being is a noble protagonist in an unfolding drama. His every gesture can have significance. He is made manifest through gestures, movement, action—*response* to the reality he encounters. His accumulated artifacts, institutions, systems, community forms, and works of art—fruits of his capacity to be at leisure with himself and others—become culture: the context and content for the formation of other persons.

Your capacity as a person to be in-formed, influenced, in-dwelt is your glory. Creation is realized through your knowing. Other persons are realized through life in community with you. Christ is realized by your subordination of all reality—all that is, all that you are—to the surpassing greatness of knowing, serving, loving God in His Church. Blessed Mother Teresa said, "God is in love with us and keeps giving Himself to the world—through you, through me." You are the place where Christ encounters the particular set of realities you face, and you voice His response.

Christians are like "pixels" of Christ, being more and more fully developed into a high-resolution image of Him. Reality that has come into the world to transform and liberate it is so far beyond the world's capacity to receive that, to human eyes, it develops slowly, over time. What has been accomplished is also being accomplished. One day it will have been perfectly accomplished, or fully realized. Until that day, we see only its partial realization—a low-resolution image, a trace of the One who is perfect in His own being.

To see yourself, you must look into a mirror, but a two-dimensional mirror cannot reflect you truly. What are you to do? You must find a very different mirror—a person! Only another person can reflect a human being, and most of us don't do it perfectly. All of us are limited in capacity to perceive being, to resonate with it, and to reflect it back into the world. Mary—perfect, pure, full of Christ—is the best example of a person as a mirror for all the being, all the reality that she encounters.

In music, resolution is progression from dissonance to consonance—the restoration of harmony. In physics, the word takes on another layer of meaning. The resolution of sunlight into its spectral colors is "prismatic resolution." Mary is the lens through which Christ gazes upon His bride, the Church, so as to see all her constituent parts, all her pixels, resolved into individual, nondetachable parts of His own image.

Beauty is the measure of truth. Any other message you accept about yourself is a lie. Mary is the gold standard for mirrors! Any mirror—a piece of glass or another person—that cannot reflect back the truth to you is simply not good enough to tell you about yourself. Those who tell teens, for instance, that they are incapable of purity are lying to them. An anorexic girl believes she is seeing "objective truth" in the mirror that calls her fat and ugly, but she is looking into a false mirror.

Resolution is also the capacity of the eye to distinguish between

32 – The Human Person

two sources of light. There is a light in which you are beautiful and a light in which you are not. Scripture tells us there can be a light within us that is darkness—a seeming reality that obscures the truth, an anti-illumination that is like a black hole. You must not only believe truth over lies but also go to a true witness for testimony about yourself—not to the "accuser," the "father of lies."

You are beautiful. Your very *being* points to the Father's love for you and delight in you. The One who created you is being realized in the world through you. Slowly, as you are purified, cleansed, healed, and polished, His image is gradually made manifest. Until then, persons are in what Mother Teresa called "distressing disguises." But His image is there, is emerging, is beautiful.

When you look into Satan's mirror, all the spots of sin you see seem to fit right in. It's hard to separate what is passing from what truly belongs—hard to view that person you see as lovable. The light within you is darkness. When you look into Mary's eyes—into the gaze of love—you see a beauty with smudges that need to be cleaned away. Beheld—held in the gaze of love—you see not one "truth" divorced from the whole reality but rather the reality that the beauty of you is becoming, is the truest thing about, your being.

The loving gaze kindles the light of truth within you and sets you free from unreality. It will help you set others free, as you learn to imitate Mary's gentle, maternal, patient opening to the being of the people you encounter. This gaze is both open and veiled. To be seen "through love" is to be seen in the light of someone's conscious choice not merely to see objective, stark reality but to see with reference to Christ's love and personhood. The one who loves is willing to be affected by the imperfect image that results, and does not demand to know every detail of the beloved. Love "covers all wrongs"—not to believe lies but to spare the beloved the full impact of exposure.

Blessed Pope John Paul said that you are the "unique, irreplaceable, unrepeatable presentation of the face of God for the people of your lifetime." God chose to mediate His presence into the world through us. We are real, becoming fully realized, *and* aiming for a destiny in which we will finally have been perfectly realized in the wholeness of all our dimensions. Time—temporal life—limits our capacity to comprehend this fullness of being in ourselves, in others, in Christ. The three-dimensionality of personhood can be expressed as development over time.

Another way to express that threefold realization of personhood is as growth from essence to specificity. The essentials of personhood are common to us all, and the specifics emerge gradually, differentiating us from one another. A child is less differentiated, and the way of the child, or the earliest stage of development in any growth, is the simple presence. In spirituality, this is manifested as a beautiful simplicity of trust in God, of waiting upon Him, of listening with docility.

As you grow up, you become more "effectively human." All the essential dignity of personhood is present in any human being, regardless of whether he has any ability to wield himself or contribute to society or have an effect in the world. But when a person *can* grow in abilities, skills, and infrastructure, he becomes more effective. Thus, the way of youth is the struggle to build the self in virtues appropriate to human being, or to some subset of knowledge or ability.

We spend most of our lives in this sort of struggle. Your own being seems to extend into a widening circle. Just as the Jews were bound by law to bless the foreigners and non-Jews in their midst, the law that is in you is meant to have an effect upon the world around you. An effect is a distinctive impression, an influence, a consequence, a result. Christ, as He is formed within you and realized through you, brings about change—order, justice, unity, restoration, reconciliation—in the home, the organizations, the neighborhood you inhabit. This occurs as you work to appropriate His teachings and then respond freely.

When you are asked to act, you go one step beyond merely being present to a reality, and you face the tension of deciding how to respond. One aspect of the reality of any situation is *you*—how you are affected, what you are feeling, what you need, what your intuition is telling you. For your response to be effective, your judgment must be informed by your heart's wisdom. Stop and consider this second dimension.

If you act hastily and forget to turn the encounter into an

encounter with Christ, then you'll probably have some regrets. Your own eyes may miss significant elements. For a three-dimensional decision, you need to invite Christ to share in the experience, to share His perspective, His wisdom. Your response is most free when the Holy Spirit brings about a creative resolution of tension within you—playing on the tensed strings you offer so as to sing a new song through you.

The goal of growing up—in life, in any area of study or skill—is to be free. Fulton Sheen said, "Free will is a gift, but freedom is a conquest." To grow in freedom, practice this full cycle over and over: be present to reality in simple understanding of what is external to you; be affected by reality, taking into account your interior dimension; respond freely once the Spirit moves you toward a particular action. Father Giussani calls this moment of forming a resolution to act the "judgment with the beat of the heart." Then, as you act in freedom, your sphere of response-ability—your freedom—grows.

The third dimension, then, is this specificity, this particular action in response to a particular reality through you—a particular person. As you learn to be at rest, childlike, at leisure, you become more essentially human. As you develop the strength to bear tension and the skill to engage in struggle, discomfort, hard work, and limitation, you become more effectively human. As you learn to respond, to utter your own judgment, to act, you become more specifically human.

Blessed Pope John Paul emphasized the "radical specificity" of the human person when he called us each to become who we are. Souls at work are persons collaborating in this work of their own becoming.

Appendix A:
Enchanting Education

Charlotte Interviews Stratford Caldecott

Stratford's books Beauty for Truth's Sake *and* Beauty in the Word *are must-reads for parents and educators who would respond in a positive and profoundly Catholic way to the educational crises of our times. Rather than expound upon all that is deeply flawed in the systems of education that prevail, he invites readers to base new creative ventures on a rich heritage of encounter with Reality. I cannot thank him enough for contributing to this work, written by one of his biggest fans.*

Father Giussani speaks of the "risk of education." What risks do you think need to be taken in the education of a child?

> The risk we take is that the child may question and ultimately disagree with us. There is a place in education for "learning by heart" and for the authority of the teacher, whose role and office is always worthy of respect, just as there is a role for training in certain important practical skills, which must be taught by a master, but in the end the purpose of education is to free the mind to such a degree that the pupil can contemplate the truth directly. The child must outgrow the teacher. Thus the teacher—and this may happen at any time and in unexpected ways, not just on graduation day—may be asked to learn from the pupil. In the book I ask whether education should be centered on the child or on the teacher, on learning or teaching, and I conclude that child and teacher must be viewed as persons-in-relation, and so the correct balance is one in which the relationship between them is given its due.

Where, in education, does/should a student practice the exercise of his or her freedom?

> "Freedom" is not just for playtime or break, although playing is an essential part of education. In a sense the goal of education—

certainly the goal of a liberal arts education, which begins in kindergarten—is the growth in freedom, both intellectual and spiritual, that comes from knowing the truth. It is the truth that sets us free. Or at least, through learning the truth—about the world, about ourselves—we gain a more important kind of freedom than any we acquire by, let's say, increased mobility, or more shelves in the supermarket. So our education, which leads us out of ourselves, or beyond ourselves (the word *e-ducere* means "leading out"), is all the time leading us into a wider world, a greater freedom.

It is very important to apply this also to ethics, to the moral development of the child. We grow up these days to think freedom is all about choice. I saw an advertising billboard the other day, announcing "Freedom is Choice." But that's not quite true. We can have all the choices in the world and not be free, if we are not strong enough to choose the right thing, the thing that will make us happy in the long term. Real freedom is this inner power to make a moral choice and stick with it—the very old word for that power is "virtue." The moral education of a child is the way he or she grows in real freedom. If freedom is simply choice, and it doesn't matter what choice as long as it's ours, then all of traditional morality looks like a set of restrictions or obstacles to our freedom, because it tells us we can do this but not that. But the right way of seeing it is to realize that having a strong moral code, and having integrity in the way we live it, is the way we grow in freedom. So freedom grows not just with truth, but with goodness, and in fact truth and goodness go together. The further you travel towards the one, the closer you get to the other.

The school tends to become a community for the child, but not for the family as a whole. What problems does this cause, and can you suggest remedies?

The Church rightly teaches that the parents are and should be the first teachers of the child, and that the family is the first school of humanity, just as it is the first cell of society. The responsibility of the parents for the education of the child continues for many years, but there is a tendency in the case of parents who send their child to school (I'm not talking about homeschoolers here) to rely on the institution to supply everything, and not even to

Appendix A: Enchanting Education

inquire what is being taught, and how. The parent may feel unable, whether for lack of time or lack of expertise, to enter into that process. In extreme cases this means allowing the State to educate or even indoctrinate the child. In any case, the separation between home and school is potentially unhealthy for both child and family. Naturally there will be dysfunctional or troubled families where everyone would agree it is a good thing for the school to take over the responsibility for the child's education from the parents. And naturally, too, where the school belongs to the parish the problem of separation may be overcome to some extent. But in general I would say it is important for the parents where possible at least to take an interest in the child's schooling, to try to follow what is being taught, and to supply what seems to be lacking, rather than allow the two worlds—that of home and of school—to become completely separated, as if they were different worlds. If the parent loves the child this interest will happen naturally, but it needs to be allowed for and encouraged. The school should help parents to know what is going on with their child, and to become actively involved if this is at all feasible.

In *Beauty for Truth's Sake*, you call us to live the liturgical year more fully, as an immersion in the cosmic order that underlies mathematics, geometry, and the arts. What are the implications of this focus on liturgical time for our design of Catholic schools?

Of course it has huge implications for the design of the school, and of the curriculum. A friend of mine once said of the tabernacle in the church that if you insert the Eucharist into a wall, the wall should change. Things should be so ordered as to emphasize or "teach" the presence of the Lord in that space. Similarly with time. The structure of our day should give a central importance to times of prayer, and our week be structured around the Sabbath. We should live partly in liturgical time—conscious of the feasts and seasons of the Church and the saints' days. In a Catholic school the same is true. Without trying to force belief where there is none, opportunities for prayer and visual reminders of God should be everywhere. These can be quite subtle. In the book I argue that architecture and even geometry are a visual language. As such they can be used to convey a religious meaning, or a secular one. Most school buildings are designed to convey a secular world-view. I am not saying that you can make the school more Catholic just by adding a few pointed arches or some symbolic decoration, but traditional societies knew how important it is to surround people with reminders of heaven or of their sacred stories. We have largely forgotten this because our civilization is very cerebral, very word-oriented, very abstracted. We should look for ways to nourish the Catholic or sacramental imagination without inducing a kind of spiritual claustrophobia in the non-religious. Beauty is the key—if we try to make things beautiful the job is well on the way to being done. And don't be fooled by that old saying that beauty is in the eye of the beholder, even if it was Shakespeare who said it first. We may have different tastes and respond to beauty in different ways, but there is something objective about it as well, something universal, and that can be demonstrated.

Parents without a rich, Catholic, classical, musical education do not have time (during childbearing years!) to reclaim or re-create it for themselves. Can they learn alongside their children, or should they turn things over to the better educated?

We are always learning, though perhaps it gets more difficult as we get older. Lack of time for formal study doesn't matter that much. We learn other things—we might be learning how to cope with stress, how to manage time, how to pray in the midst of a busy life, and so on. Let's hope we can always grow in wisdom! Having children, even just observing them, and of course interacting with them, accommodating ourselves to their needs, creating a healthy ethos in the home, these things are ways that we learn. Following as best we can the things our children are learning in school, this is also an opportunity for us. The key thing is not to renounce all responsibility just because we don't feel well-enough educated ourselves. We can always be involved to some degree, and if our children see in us the kind of humility that is prepared to listen to a teacher even as an adult, that can be an object-lesson for them too.

Great liturgy is great education. How much damage can be done by poor liturgy? How can parents respond positively and protectively when liturgy seems to fight against the formation of their kids?

Appendix A: Enchanting Education

Liturgy is a school for our humanity. But as you say it can be done badly—even if there are no actual abuses, and the official rubrics are observed to the letter, there can be a lack of attention, a lack of true reverence, a pomposity or coldness, that is off-putting and communicates the wrong message especially to the young, who are sensitive to these things. In some cases the experience of bad liturgy can turn someone against the practice of their faith. Catholics need to defend their liturgy, especially from abuses, and it is our right to insist that things are done properly. But the most important thing, even when reacting against a legitimate grievance, is to be in the right spirit oneself—not a spirit that is self-righteous or contentious, arrogant or harsh, but one that is gentle and respectful, humble and prudent. Arguments over liturgy can divide a parish against itself, and make the church a battleground. That can't be right. And of course we have to remember that tastes differ, and that looking at the liturgy to criticize it is not going to help anyone to pray. If the Mass is valid, even if it is a bit of a mess (a priest I knew used to end his celebration with words that sounded like "The Mess is ended"), nevertheless Christ is present and grace is flowing from heaven. It is up to the Church to offer the Mass correctly; it is up to us to learn and to teach the right way to participate and to receive.

You've said that all subjects should be taught with a sense of their story—the history of the subject's development. Many of us parents and teachers have a weakness in this area. Do you have recommendations for books—upper elementary, let's say—to help us teach children this way?

Well, I wouldn't be too rigid about this, but I wanted to make the point that every subject—every science and every art, let's say—does have a history. It doesn't just drop from the sky. And often learning the human story of how certain discoveries were made, how the subject has evolved through time and what it tells us about our humanity and our culture, add to the fascination of the subject itself. I thought that might be the case particularly with mathematics, for example, which many young people (myself included) have found off-putting when it is presented as a highly abstract set of rules and formulae to be learned by heart and applied to problems. A more interesting way into the subject is to be shown how mathematics is a process of discovery, in which each breakthrough is a creative response to a challenge, and each builds on those that came before. There is a human story to be told about math and geometry, and it may be that this will help to engage a child's imagination more effectively than a purely abstract presentation. It's a strategy, anyway. And the same kind of thing is true of other subjects. In this way, too, we build up the understanding of our own culture and tradition that Christopher Dawson thought was so important.

There are dangers to systematizing education, and dangers to unschooling. What counsel do you have for those designing courses, programs, and schools regarding how much structured vs. free time to allow?

Be intelligent about it! And be sensitive to the situation you find yourself in, and the people you are working with. I have no intention of proposing an ideological solution, or a simple recipe for a "good" education. I just wanted to develop an approach that would respect what we know, as Catholics, about the human person. That is to say, the human person as called to fulfillment in love, and as having a "right" to be loved. And the human person as fundamentally curious, desirous of truth, responsive to beauty, possessing a moral conscience. If we get that right, we are off to a good start, and we have a better basis on which to build an educational system.

We know a lot about the dangers of media and computer use. What do you think about the place of computer use and development of computer skills in the curriculum? (*Side note: I know of a school that gives every student a computer, and the geometry class is all done on computers . . . no compass, no proofs, no constructions!*)

Computers are another area where we need to be intelligent! It is so easy to throw technology into the classroom in a way that will have a disastrous effect on education. I talk about this a bit in *Beauty in the Word*. Computers can make us stupid—or rather, reliance on computers makes us stupid. The availability of calculators deprives us of the opportunity to learn how calculations are made. Mobile phones in class distract us in ways that seriously damage our ability to learn. Education, as I try to argue, is largely about paying attention—the child paying attention to the teacher and the subject, the teacher paying attention to the child. Computers and other technologies have to be integrated into the educational setting in a way that does not undermine that quality of attention.

What do you think of all-day kindergarten? Year-round schooling, or 180-day schooling? Preschool? Twelve-year college prep education? What portion of a day, year, life should formal education occupy?

I don't feel able to go into that level of detail just yet. I would want to listen to the experience of parents and teachers first. The books I wrote were supposed to prepare the philosophical ground for the next phase of the project, a stage of listening and consulting that would lead in turn to the production of some practical resources for schools. Among other things, we want to give some attention and exposure to examples of good practice in education, experiments that have succeeded, new schools that seem to be getting things right—so that others can draw upon this experience.

There is so much to teach, and so little time! You've described a wealth of story, poetry, drama, sacred geometry, life skills, math, history, science, literature, theology, and more. It is all so important, and our kids are growing past the "right stages" so fast. How can we approach this all without anxiety, pressure, fear?

I would say that it is important to realize three things. First, that we are never going to get everything right. We just have to try to do the best we can with the materials and circumstances available to us. Second, that children are more resilient than we think, and education is not something we have to do to the child but something the child will do for himself or herself with our help (and sometimes without us). It is a matter of kindling an interest that, once sparked, will grow into a blaze, drawing fuel to itself. The third is that, as Catholics or just as religious believers, we know that God cares for and guides each human soul, and so—thank goodness!—whatever we succeed in doing or fail to do, the child's fate is not entirely dependent on us.

What deficiencies have you had to overcome in your own education? If you could master one skill you don't currently possess, what would it be? Why?

> I was fortunate in many ways—in my parents, and in the schooling I received—and yet inevitably there were deficiencies and gaps. I have learned a great deal from my family, especially my wife. Leonie is a great mother and teacher, as well as writer. A lot of what I write comes from her, or what I have learned from seeing her in action. But in terms of specific gaps in my education, I never got the hang of music theory, and also I regret not mastering mathematics. In that case it was out of a reluctance to keep asking the "stupid" questions. Instead I kept quiet and pretended to understand when I didn't, or learned the methods for getting the right answers without really comprehending the principles involved. And I regret not learning other languages, perhaps at an earlier age when they are said to be easier to acquire. I am sure a mastery of several languages is a great help in life, and a great enrichment. But I am grateful for what I did manage to learn, and to the many good teachers who helped me. I wish in later years I had gone back to thank them—I'm sure many teachers never know what an impact they have had, and how much good they have done.

In *Beauty in the Word* you say the human person should be educated for imagination, among other things. Please tell us more about how to educate for imagination.

> Imagination comes naturally to children, unless it is beaten out of them in some way. So we educate for imagination simply by giving it some encouragement. The best stimulus, of course, is for the parents to read stories to the child from an early age—as soon as possible. Then we encourage children to play, to explore, to invent games. We play with them, if we are able. In a more formal setting, use drama, music, dance, poetry, storytelling, mime, to teach parts of the curriculum, or integrate those methods into the teaching. Take the children, if you can, to see things and places that will fuel their imagination, even if it is only a field trip in the park, sketching plants, or a visit to the museum, looking for their favorite object and then talking about it to the class. Bring in a guest speaker or two, to tell about their experiences. Encourage children to talk to old people, even to "interview"

them, to find out what the world used to be like. When teaching history, try to bring it alive, help them to see that history is all about real people and what they chose to do, and what happened to them as a result. Don't be afraid of fairy tales and mythology. G. K. Chesterton in his book *Orthodoxy* writes about the truth that is in such stories.

What is a good approach to dealing with error—non-Catholic belief systems, heresies, disputes among Catholics, apologetics—during our dialectic and rhetoric phases of education? How can we equip the kids to think through to Truth without confusing them?

First, you spoke of the Trivium as a series of "phases"—Grammar, Logic or Dialectic, Rhetoric—and that comes from the famous essay by Dorothy L. Sayers called "The Lost Tools of Learning." Certainly that is a helpful way of thinking about it. The child does go through these developmental stages. But there is another sense in which the child never outgrows Grammar, never outgrows Logic.* That's just a footnote here, although it's important in the book. But your main question is very challenging. How do we present the possibility of error, and heresy? We are trying gradually to enable children to think for themselves: does this mean we don't teach them what we know as true? I think Sayers was right that at a certain (early) stage, children aren't much interested in being presented with lots of alternative views; they just want to know what's the case, and they are looking for someone to teach them "with authority." They are trying to orient themselves. Clearly this should be the role of the parent, in the first instance—to give the child a world-view and a framework, a sense of direction, of right and wrong. And then we have the Church. As Catholics we are on solid ground when we say that these things in the Catechism are true, and these other things are not. We never outgrow the Catechism or the Creed—instead we grow into them. But it's no secret that some drop away, and that many adopt other views. As the child becomes aware of alternate points of view, different ideas of truth, it is important that we convey that we believe what we do not just out of habit or fear, but because there are good rational reasons to

---

* *Amen! This is the thesis of* Souls at Work!

accept the authority of the Church as the guardian of revealed truth—despite all the scandals, all the accusations that children will inevitably hear. We mustn't split faith from reason. We have to be able to show that reason grows alongside faith and that both are needed, and that they help each other (as Pope John Paul II says in *Fides et Ratio*).

In joining with other parents, or with a school, I give up flexibility, individualized instruction, some authority over curriculum and philosophy. What do I gain?

> You gain the resources of an institution to help educate your child, including experienced teachers. The child maybe gains a set of friends and experiences they wouldn't otherwise have had. And you gain all those hours in the day when they are in school!

In homeschooling, I place demands on myself for continuing education, judgments as to philosophy and curriculum, investment of time. What do I gain?

> The things you learn from teaching them. And the closeness: all those hours, months, years of your child's life that a school would have stolen from you!

What questions would you ask about a teacher before placing a child in his or her classroom?

> Why did they go into teaching? What do they get out of it? Do they like children?

Catholic schools usually require university-trained, state-certified teachers whose education in pedagogy and in an understanding of the human person has been, at best, non-Catholic and, at worst, anti-Catholic. Where are Catholic teachers being trained to teach and to help develop schools along the lines you describe in *Beauty for Truth's Sake* and *Beauty in the Word*?

> I wish I could say, "All over the place," but I can't. In England, the Maryvale Institute in Birmingham does a good job giving teachers a Catholic formation. In the US, I have the impression there are several good programs. But I haven't done the research on this yet. Up to now, my interest has been primarily in developing a theory of education, and practical applications have had to wait. I'd be interested to hear if anyone knows.

Appendix A: Enchanting Education

Your books are the kind of "rhetoric" that invites conversation, opens dialogue, asks leading questions. Your readers from all over the world are letting you know about their new educational models, experiments, and ideas. Can you tell us about some of the most promising?

> Well, we're still only at the beginning of this process. I am sure as the book circulates we'll get many more people writing to us. In the book I refer to St. Jerome's Academy in Hyattsville, which I think—if things continue to go well—could be a kind of model for schools of the future. I also recently found out about the plans of the Clairvaux Institute to establish St. Gregory's Academy in Scranton. That sounds extremely promising! And there are lots of other green shoots around. Dale Ahlquist of the American Chesterton Society has founded a school, as has the C.S. Lewis Foundation, and I was recently in Italy where the Chestertonians have also now founded an independent cooperative school. Of course there are also several small liberal arts colleges that are worth watching, including St. Thomas More College in New Hampshire which has recently reformed its curriculum in interesting ways. Meanwhile the Benedictus Trust wants to create the first Catholic liberal arts college in the UK, though it is still seeking support. My own book *Beauty in the Word* was commissioned by a group in England that aims to produce a number of resources for the reform of Catholic education in the coming years. Other projects are perhaps still too embryonic to mention here. As I find out about things I will make sure to list them on my blog so that others can see what is out there. We need to pool our ideas and experience, and the blog is obviously a useful instrument for doing that.
>
> http://beauty-in-education.blogspot.co.uk

Appendix B

The Questionnaire: Charlotte Interviews SAW Readers

The Tensions section of Souls at Work *was developed with the collaboration of a number of people who graciously responded to a series of questions I posed. I pose them here, for your group study or journaling. I was gratified by the respondents who thanked me for the opportunity to reflect on and articulate aspects of their own formation. I hope my readers will also enjoy that experience.*

Education vs. Formation

1. What is "education"?
2. What is "formation"?
3. What experiences are you aware of that have shaped your soul—positively or negatively—or have had an impact on your spiritual growth?
4. Please describe whatever formal education you've had.
5. What was/is the effect of your education on your spiritual life?
6. Please describe how you have been educated about religious or spiritual things.
7. How has media (television, movies, Internet) helped educate you?
8. How would you describe yourself as a student? (A-student, dropout, slacker, passive, eager beaver, etc.)
9. Please describe your current approach to spiritual life and growth.
10. Have you ever experienced God forming/teaching/changing/shaping you without your conscious participation? Please describe the experience(s).

Appendix B

Work vs. Leisure

1. Please describe the work you do.
2. What training, credentials, ongoing investment, physical capabilities, and skills does your work demand?
3. Does your daily work correspond to a vocation from God?
4. What things besides your work are parts of your "identity"?
5. How do you typically spend Sundays?
6. Please describe whatever understanding you have of "holy leisure" or "keeping the Sabbath holy."
7. What "work" are you currently doing on yourself, to become more "you" or to improve "you"?
8. Please describe how your life is "in balance" or "not in balance."
9. Please describe how your daily work is or is not satisfying.
10. What are the top ten things you would do if you were completely free to do whatever you wanted?

Child vs. Adult

1. What was childhood like for you?
2. Do you remember what got your attention, what you were interested in, as a child?
3. Have you pursued childhood interests, or have they been set aside?
4. Are there any children in your life right now? (Please tell about how much time you get to spend with children and whether they're your own, students, friends' kids, etc.)
5. When you spend time with children, what do you enjoy, and what do you dislike about "kid time"?
6. Do you ever sketch or paint what you see? Please tell about the kind of artwork you do, subjects, media.
7. What are the three greatest struggles or tensions in your adult life?
8. What have you had to give up as you've grown older?

9. What does it feel like to you to be moving toward old age?
10. When do you feel like a little kid again?

Freedom vs. Form

1. What is the hardest lesson you've ever learned?
2. If you could master one skill (one you don't already possess), what would it be? Why?
3. Have you ever experienced any form of paralysis? Please describe the situation and how it felt to be "powerless."
4. Have you ever made what you later considered to be a completely *wrong* move, a *ridiculous* decision, a self-deluded choice? Please describe it/them.
5. How is your current life affected by or constrained by choices you've made in the past?
6. Do you ever wish you had less freedom? Please describe when/why.
7. What kinds of boundaries are you operating within right now? Are they firm or flexible limits? Did you choose them, or are they "givens"?
8. Can you think of any sense in which you can identify with those who reject the teachings of the Church or her rules, rites, or obligations?
9. How do you express (communicate, give, show, represent) your essential self, your unique you-ness, to others? From whom do you withhold this?
10. What are you currently struggling to learn? What makes it so hard?

Art vs. Intellect

1. How "intellectual" are you, and how do you know?
2. What is your greatest intellectual weakness (memory, mathematics, history, language, science… use whatever categories make sense to you) and how do you know?

Appendix B

3. Would you identify yourself as a "visual learner," a "verbal learner," a "kinesthetic learner," a "poetic or artistic learner," a person with "mechanical intelligence," or as any other type of learner that makes sense to you? And, again, how do you know?
4. What are your credentials? (Licenses, degrees, professional certifications, titles, references, etc.)
5. Please describe any creative experience you have had—in the arts, starting businesses, solving problems, whatever you've done that you consider to have involved "creativity."
6. Have you had any formal training in the arts? Please describe it.
7. How/why are "intellectuals" in danger of compromising their faith or spiritual lives?
8. How/why are "artists" in danger of compromising their faith or spiritual lives?
9. Please describe how your intellectual and artistic development has contributed to or detracted from your own spiritual growth.
10. Please describe your imagination—is it a place you spend much time in? Do you struggle to control it? Is it full of things you wish to contemplate, or wish would go away? Does it easily take you to other places/times/scenes that feel very real? Is it strong, weak, active, unused, valuable, helpful, disciplined, dangerous, delightful, painful? (Remember, this is your own imagination, not the imagination in general.)

Individual vs. Community

1. What proportion of your waking hours do you spend in the company of other people?
2. Of your in-company time, what proportion is spent with family only? With single individuals, or small and intimate groups? With small interest- or need-based groups (your alcoholics anonymous meeting or the Brewers Guild, for instance)? In formal instruction or class situations? In formal religious situations (Mass, spiritual direction, prayer sodalities, confession,

RCIA, etc.)? In public situations (shopping malls, traffic, airports, laundromats, etc.)?

3. If you categorized your time as "private" and "public" instead of "alone" and "with people," what proportion of your time is spent privately vs. publicly?

4. What proportion of your time with family is spent at leisure, and what proportion is spent in more of a "task" orientation? (It's completely up to you whether you think "driving to Church," for instance, is a leisurely or task-oriented time with your kids; cooking dinner might be a task to accomplish, or you may perceive it as a time of leisure… you get the idea: answer according to your subjective sense of things.)

5. What proportion of your time with spouse and close friends is spent at leisure, and what proportion is spent in a more task-oriented way? (Again, for example, a book study with friends may be a task-oriented activity for you or a leisurely one… it's your subjective sense of things.)

6. What proportion of your time alone is spent at leisure, and what proportion is spent with a task orientation? (Once again, your commitment to exercise, for example, might feel like a task or like taking time to play… it's your call.)

7. What proportion of your time with non–family members is spent in your home or in theirs? Where else do you get together with others?

8. What proportion of your time is spent in pursuit of your own education, or formation, or skill-building (your piano practice, your book study group, your spiritual direction, your reading, etc.)? Is most of this "public" or "private" time?

9. What would you like to work on learning, if you could find a friend or group of friends to do it with you?

10. What would you like to work on learning, if you could be alone to focus on it by yourself?

Church vs. Culture

1. What activities, traditions, practices that are part of your life really "define" your family "culture"? You might compare/con-

Appendix B

trast your family's culture with that of some other family you know or view your family through the eyes of someone from a foreign culture.

2. What cultural activities do you enjoy (out in the wider world... not just your own family's culture, but interacting with others) that are "Catholic"? How about those you enjoy that are "not Catholic"?

3. What aspects of the secular culture are compatible with your faith?

4. What aspects of the secular culture are incompatible with your faith?

5. Have you "baptized" any secular activities—added Catholic elements, practices, significance to otherwise nonreligious events or elements of culture? (For example, the annual neighborhood Fourth of July parade to which you add a Catholic prayer in the home before participating, or putting holy cards instead of candy into trick-or-treaters' bags, or taking St. somebody's picture to work as patron saint of your profession... or whatever you can think of!)

6. Have you adapted any Catholic cultural elements to secular life, or adjusted them so that they accommodate participation by people of other faiths? (For example, saying your dinner grace without the sign of the cross when Protestant grandma is present... you get the idea!)

7. Please describe the various "cultures" in which you spend your time (family, ethnic neighborhood, workplace, Internet communities, etc.). How do age, ethnicity, income, religion, education, nationality, gender, and special interests create/affect the cultures that form your context? Are you active in creating/affecting these cultures, or are they pretty much "givens" for you? Are they hostile to your faith, neutral, or encouraging?

8. Please think of a "teaching situation" you recall (for example, you were learning or teaching the Faith, or something else that is important to you). How were you, or those you taught, prepared by your (or their) dominant cultural experiences to receive, or reject, or understand what was being taught? How did this preparation affect the way the material needed to be

taught? Please describe the way culture and education interconnected in this experience.

9. To whom are you "alien" because of big cultural differences? Who is "alien" to you? (This is more than just "having differences"—it is truly feeling like you come from different worlds or are having serious trouble with even basic interaction, understanding, empathy, and identification.)

10. Please give examples of someone going "too far" in being "countercultural." How about examples of someone going "too far" in being in line with or accommodating a culture? The culture you are thinking of might be religious, ethnic, age-oriented… any of the categories we've been looking at. Your "counter" and "accommodating" examples might refer to different cultures or to the same culture.

Safety vs. Risk

1. Please describe some of the risks you've been exposed to in the course of your life and how they (or your responses to them) have affected and formed you.

2. How have you been protected from dangers? How have the protective actions/structures/strategies/substances affected you?

3. What dangers have you sought actively or chosen freely? What were the results or ramifications?

4. What is your approach to "error" or to dangerous beliefs and teachings? Can you give some examples? (For instance, how you deal with those who question your faith; how you handle dialogue with people whose beliefs seem "alien" or false; whether you seek out, study, and respond to the opposition's position; whether or not you read books by people you consider wrongheaded; how you limit your exposure to falsehood and diabolical influence.)

5. How is this approach (to error, above) different when it comes to protecting/teaching children, students, or anyone weaker (in regard to faith, intellect, maturity, etc.) than yourself? How were you helped (or, how do you help your children) to move from childhood's to adulthood's approach?

Appendix B

6. How comfortable are you with debate, conflict, or argument? Does it make a difference what the topic is? Or who the "opponent" is? Please give examples of situations from your own experience.

7. How comfortable are you with emotional vulnerability (for example, exposing faults, expressing your feelings, crying openly, asking for/accepting forgiveness, reconciling with someone who has hurt you)? What factors increase or decrease your willingness to take emotional risk? Please give examples from your experience.

8. In what ways are you exposed, or do you expose yourself, to the scrutiny/feedback/judgment/authority of others? (For example, performance review, spiritual direction, accountability groups, track coach, going over monthly budget with spouse.) How has criticism, or your response to it, affected and formed you?

9. Please give examples of times when you've completely changed your mind; when you've been proved dead wrong; when you've realized that your position's foundation was weak; when you've "seen the light."

10. If you ranked all your beliefs/judgments/opinions on a scale from 10 ("absolute/unshakable confidence") to 1 ("lightly held /very open to new evidence or influence"), what would be some of your 10s? 5s? 1s? What does it take to move from 1 to 10? What kinds of evidence/proof/feelings/authority increase your confidence and undergird your 10s?

Intention vs. Attention

1. What are some of the things that compete for your attention? Which most often win?

2. What are some of the things you'd like to pay more attention to? How do they get shut out? What good things refuse to clamor for your attention or seem to stay hidden "in the background"?

3. How often do you act/move/speak without having a clear intention first? (Reaction vs. proaction.) Please describe a situ-

ation in which you did form a clear intention first, and how that was different for you, had different results, etc.

4. Please give examples of things that have attracted you toward a deep, absorbing interest in them.

5. How aware are you of your body's health, posture, pain, needs, desires, imbalance, and limits? Do you think you'd be better off with less or more awareness of this kind?

6. How do you respond to your own feelings? If you are sad? Fearful? Angry? Needy? How are you loving or unloving to yourself?

7. Have you ever formed a clear intention and then been unable to act on it, or execute it, or realize the idea? What interfered or impeded? How did you deal with it? What did you learn to do differently next time? How did the phase of "powerlessness" feel?

8. What ideas that circulate in your mind do not become intentions to act? Are you consciously inhibiting response to negative ideas? Are you unconsciously failing to cultivate response to positive ideas? Are some of the ideas so vague that they stimulate neither form of self-control?

9. Are you able to form vivid imaginations that actually stimulate an emotional response? Are you able to shut down imaginary scenarios and "mental movies" that you consider vain, impure, counterproductive, or a waste of time?

10. What role does distraction play in your life? Do you seek out distraction (and if so, from what)? Is distraction sometimes a coping mechanism (and if so, for what stresses)? Do you have trouble with interference from unwanted distractions or from a condition (such as ADHD) that affects your ability to deal with stimulus/response well? What attracts your attention in a positive way? In a negative way?

Delight vs. Discipline

1. What are some ways you practice self-discipline? Is practice gradually "making perfect"?

Appendix B

2. What would be lost if you tossed your personal disciplines to the wind and just did whatever felt delightful? What would be gained?

3. What are the organizing structures of your life (for example, schedules, files, Google Calendar, workplace hours and rules, school hours and rules, church requirements, organization systems and procedures, habits, physical order of environment)? Who designed these? How are they evaluated for effectiveness? How do they free or constrain you?

4. Give examples of disciplines that have led to freedom or delight or have become pleasant in themselves. Were they very hard, or unpleasant, or costly to develop?

5. Which of your self-disciplines began as an external demand, law, or constraint? Which ones have you imposed upon yourself?

6. What is your interior response to discipline? Does it make a difference whether it is an external or internal imposition? What "helps the medicine go down" more easily?

7. If you were completely free to choose, what disciplines or organization structures or constraints would you eliminate?

8. If you were completely free to choose, what abilities, delights, freedoms would you pursue?

9. How can desire lead you toward your true self, your highest destiny, God, truth? How can desire mislead you? How can you judge whether to follow your own desires?

10. In what ways do you wield yourself so as to get/do what you want? In what ways do you yield yourself so as to accomplish what God wants?

Appendix C:
The Form of Sabbath

IN *Souls at Rest: An Exploration of the Eucharistic Sabbath*, I invited readers to enter into the form of the Sabbath. In light of the language of form and freedom, growth and dimensionality that I have used in *Souls at Work*, I want to recapitulate, briefly, the idea of Sabbath.

Sabbath rest, as the introduction to and the basis of a practice of holy leisure, is to the work of crafting a life what the pro-gymnasium is to the trivium of classical education: a deeply poetic, experiential preparation. Centered on the provision of "every good gift" in the Eucharist, Sabbath-keeping is a practice that cultivates the capacity to more and more fully receive that gift. *Souls at Rest* corresponds to the way of the child, to poetic knowledge, and to the database of lived experience and environmental formation. *Souls at Work* corresponds to the way of youth, to analytical understanding, and to the database of the use of language. *Souls at Play* (forthcoming) corresponds to the way of the adult, to synthetic wisdom, and to the database of creative response.

A childlike approach to the Sabbath day is a beautiful one. If, in simple trust and obedience, you go where Christ is in order to receive Him, then He loves to give Himself to you. When He admonished His apostles to "suffer the children to come to Him," perhaps it was because He knew their tendency would be to forget how perfect and pleasing the way of the child is to Him. Since they would be expected to move on into the tasks of maturation, they might come to despise the freedom of anyone who approached Christ in childlike simplicity.

To move into a fuller dimensionality of Sabbath-keeping, then, is in no way to suggest that some have earned the right to more of Christ. He gives His all to each one who receives Him. Again, differences in the extent to which we are able to *realize* what we have

Appendix C: The Form of Sabbath

received—to fully appropriate and understand—may be enormous, but the Gift is the same yesterday, today, and forever. As with any form, then, the movement into the way of youth is a movement into tension.

The tensions presented by the task of consciously designing your Sabbath practice are much the same as the tensions you have considered in *Souls at Work*. It will not be easy to decide what to do, what not to do, how to choose between many positive possibilities, and how to incorporate interior judgments into gestures and actions, and it will not be easy to agree with members of family and community on Sabbath practices.

The lens I hope you will look through as you work to consider and resolve such tensions is the freedom of the human person. When you craft your Sabbath, please keep in mind that it was designed to restore, support, invite, and encourage your freedom. You must take into account the particular ways in which you, personally, get de-formed or get thrown into dis-order. One person may need to stop as much activity as possible on Sundays (to provide a tonic or corrective for an overbusy life during the week), while another may need to exert himself by entering into formal prayer or giving himself in service to others (as a corrective for an ordinarily informal or self-centered weekday style).

Crafting your response to Sabbath—making a setting for the jewel of the Eucharist—expands your sphere of response-ability, the interior spaciousness of your being, your capacity for Christ, and, thus, your freedom. To move into the fullest possible experience, you will want to learn everything you can about the Faith, the Mass, the gestures and ritual of liturgy, and the people around you. Then, you'll want to invite the Holy Spirit to quicken the life of Christ in you so that you can shine that light into the world you inhabit—through forms you create: gestures, books, classes, works of art, community life, pilgrimage, and much, much more. Enjoy that journey!

Do You Need a Speaker?

CharlotteOstermann.com

Author of *Souls at Rest: An Exploration of the Eucharistic Sabbath*
and *Souls at Work: An Invitation to Freedom*

Forthcoming: *Souls at Play: A Reflection on Creativity*

Holy Leisure is the Key to Human Being!
Holy Leisure is the Key to Human Freedom!
Holy Leisure is the Key to Human Creativity!

A Few of My Talks:

Grow Up in All Things . . . . . . for RCIA, Most Pure Heart of Mary
Sabbath: As Easy as A, B, C . . . . . . for Daughters of Isabella, KCK
Beauty Becomes You . . . . . . for Blessed Sacrament Homeschoolers
Building the Bridge . . . . for KS Homeschool Conference
Hi-Resolution Beauty . . . . for Apostles of the Interior Life Retreat
3-D Transcendentals . . . . . . for Benedictine College, Atchison, KS
G.K. Chesterton on Art . . . . for Catholic Creatives Salon
The Poetic Reader . . . . for Ladies Literary Society

Milton Keynes UK
Ingram Content Group UK Ltd.
UKHW011246040324
438719UK00003B/43